Intermittently called by Christ

Piercing the Darkness.
The Autobiography of a Broken and Enlightened Man

CHARLES L. GOODEN

1

Foreword

To all who embark on the pages of "Intermittently Called
by Christ: Piercing the Darkness - The autobiography and
wisdom of a Broken and Enlightened Man," I extend my
warmest greetings and heartfelt gratitude for joining us on this
extraordinary journey. As the wife of the remarkable author,
Charles L. Gooden, I stand here with immense joy and pride
as I introduce you to a man whose life's story has been
profoundly shaped by the grace of God and the power of
unwavering faith.

This book is a testament to Charles's resilience and the
transformative power of God's love in the face of adversity. As
I've witnessed him traverse the depths of darkness and emerge
into the radiance of enlightenment, I can't help but feel deeply
moved by the profound wisdom he has gained through his
experiences. In these pages, you will discover a captivating
narrative of a man who faced hardships head-on, guided only
by the unwavering belief in a higher power.

"Intermittently Called by Christ" is a remarkable chronicle
of triumph over tribulations, and it serves as an inspiring
reminder that even in our darkest moments, we are not alone.
Charles bares his soul, revealing the vulnerable aspects of his
journey, and through his candid reflections, we come to
understand the depth of his faith and the magnitude of God's
love that has guided him through life's tumultuous storms.

As his loving wife, I have seen firsthand how these
experiences have reshaped Charles's thinking and the way he
approaches life. It is with profound gratitude that I
acknowledge the divine guidance that led him to recognize the
importance of cherishing the blessings he has received,
including the cherished bond of marriage.

Within the pages of this book, you will encounter a man whose heart is filled with gratitude for the love he has been blessed with. With humility and unwavering commitment, Charles shares how he discovered the true meaning of Ephesians 5:25, learning to love his wife with the selflessness and devotion that reflects the love of Christ for His Church.

May this powerful memoir serve as an inspiring beacon of hope and a gentle reminder that amidst life's trials, we are never alone. May it encourage you to seek solace in faith during times of struggle, trusting that God's divine plan is always at work, molding us into stronger, wiser, and more compassionate beings.

To my beloved husband, Charles, you are an extraordinary man, and I am deeply honored to walk this life journey by your side. Your unwavering faith and unyielding love for God have not only transformed your life but have also enriched mine in immeasurable ways. Your resilience and determination are a testament to the strength that lies within the human spirit when touched by the divine.

To all the readers, I hope this heartfelt memoir touches your hearts as it has touched mine. May it serve as a reminder that with faith as our guide, we can overcome any darkness that befalls us and emerge into the light, wiser and more enlightened than ever before.

With boundless love and eternal hope.

Tasha M. Gooden

Welcome

The best dream happens when we are awakened by the touch of Christ. Have you ever felt lost with no hope for tomorrow. My brief but painful experience as a child was unfortunate, I just happen to be able to escape the horror of abuse that so many have been trapped in. To overcome so many obstacles and finish my journey is a miracle. I am thankful I get to share my story of the intermittent touches of Christ in my life that helped form and freed me from the scars and sorrows of this life. As a man we have been taught to hide our feeling and that it's against the status que of what a man is supposed to represent. We live in a very perfect but imperfect world. The false perception of power based on position and status has allowed some to believe they can speak for the masses. This is further from the truth. In fact, we cannot speak unless God speaks through us in the humility and the power of His being. It is not for gain or power or status or to hold a title. We are one resource.

As a man, it wasn't until I was broken that I begin to see the light of life. We can all change; and that change doesn't come in our perfection but in our imperfection. We must be willing to accept and admit our faults despite the circumstances. To tell the truth about who we are, to discover who we are becoming in God's plan. It's impossible to see in the darkness of a world self-centered for power and status. I can only hope you gain insight from a broken and contrite spirit and gain some insight and perspective from a man that was touched by God in all his faults. Enjoy the read. Look for something positive in each day, even if some days look dark. God want you to approach life in the moment of Now. No Other Way. Being aware of your present position can and will only change when you know that life changes based on the influence of energy rather it be positive or negative frequency, thereby becoming self-fulfilling, contagious and the influence in your life and those around you. A commitment to be your best and to inspire others to be their best sets up a legacy that motivates others to respond and it is a byproduct of having and demonstrating the right attitudes. The timeless characteristics of honesty, integrity and accountability are what inspire people to trust and follow righteousness.

I believe the righteousness of Christ is an effective way to getting us on the playing field as men, with the tools needed to run the race that is set before us looking unto Christ as the leader, protector, and author of our faith. To improve our attitudes and abilities, that will positively impact our family life and those in our circle of influence. The ideas you are about to read are timeless and universal. Only you can apply them daily in life.

Why is this worth reading? Good question. I felt rejected and was mentally and physically abused. and I have done my best to fill this book with insightful, practical, and motivating insights that you can gleam from. In all your getting get an understanding first. You need to know that these ideas are not abstract concepts or esoteric, academic theology conjured up by an author who has no real-life experience. This information is about transformation, and it is meant to be shared.

Our attitude transcends what we believe. There is no special difference in a positive attitude that inspires change. You cannot change until you change. Your breakthrough will not happen in a day. You will need to embrace it in love and commitment with continuous improvement in the process. It will require a change in your thinking.

You will have to be patient, kind and walk in love and be understanding with yourself. You cannot be jealous, conceited, and proud in your thinking. You cannot be ill mannered, selfish, or irritable. You cannot keep a record of wrong things. You cannot think more of yourself than you really are. You will have to be proactive not reactive; you cannot rejoice in evil but be happy with truth, honesty, and integrity. You will need to remain steadfast, focused and committed to the vision you want for your own life.

Charles L Gooden

Legal Notice and Disclaimer:

This publication is protected under the US Copyright Act of 1976 and all other applicable international, federal, state, and local laws, and all rights are reserved, including resale rights: you are not allowed to give or sell this Guide to anyone else. Please note that much of this publication is based on personal experience and anecdotal evidence. Although the author and publisher have made every reasonable attempt to achieve complete accuracy of the content in this Guide, they assume no responsibility for errors or omissions. Also, you should use this information as you see fit, and at your own risk. Your situation may not be exactly suited to the examples illustrated here; in fact, it's likely that they won't be the same, and you should adjust your use of the information and recommendations accordingly. Any trademarks, service marks, product names or named features are assumed to be the property of their respective owners and are used only for reference. There is no implied endorsement if we use one of these terms. Finally, use your head. Nothing in this Guide is intended to replace common sense, legal, medical, or other professional advice and is meant to inform and entertain the reader. The publication is designed to provide accurate and authorized information regarding the subject matter covered. It is therefore sold with the understanding that the publisher is not engaged in rendering legal, accounting, or other professional services.

All scriptures noted are from either NIV for the Holy Bible, New international Version Copy write 1973, 1978, by International Bible society. Used by permission all rights reserved. This book is a reprint of The Purpose Driven Husband by Charles Gooden. All rights reserved. This book or any parts thereof may not be reproduced in any form without permission.

Preface

The metamorphose from a lengthy life of sex, crime and drugs in my childhood challenges the idea of the paradoxical and mysterious nature of the transfiguration from a life of sin to being a disciple of Christ, this is the key to our transformation. I began as a Teacher, Evangelist in 1984 and was first ordained as in minister of the Gospel message 1985. My reference to the bible is a transfiguration within a pattern of divine revelation that we must uncover in our daily life. God's revelation to humans, or divine revelation, is never only for knowledge but relationship. Its purpose isn't for us to only know about God. Rather, it's for us to know God, which is inherently transformational. In my intermittent touch I discovered when Christ was transfigured, or showed his divine nature to the apostles, he did so to show them that they too might be changed to become disciples of Christ. Not a figure of ego or position or status. "It is ... the duty and the privilege of all disciples of our glorified Savior, to be exalted and resurrected with Him; to live in heaven in their thoughts, motives, aims, desires, likings, prayers, praises, intercessions, even while they are in the flesh; to look like other men, to be busy like other men, to be passed over in the crowd of men, or even to be scorned or oppressed, as other men may be, but the while to have a secret channel of communication with the Most High, a gift the world knows not of; to have their life hid with Christ in God." What did it mean to me... follow Christ's transfiguration to my own transformation?

The references of Christ's transfiguration are significant. He ascends the mountain, and at the top shows his glorified nature. I saw this as the apex of Christian faith and prayer, where all is "still and calm as heaven." Yet not without the valley of uncertainties. Christ and his apostles couldn't stay at the summit of the mountain forever. They eventually had to descend the mountain and face a world that runs counter to the serenity of heaven. The world is still witnessing the ever-present descent from the mountain to the valley during an often-unforgiving world, Christ's transfiguration provides the hope of transformation. All who ascend are transformed. Those whose descent leads to dramatic change can rest assured that Christ suffers was not in vain but yielded the fruit which enables us to live and rest in the assurances if we follow Him. Those transformed in Christ will emit a special kind of light in a world, which, as we all know, is often filled with darkness. The man intermittently touched by Christ is led by the light of Christ through the holy spirit will be empowered through the often-unpleasantries of this world.

The transfiguration of the man touched changes in a very notable way, usually from a fleshly state of mind to a spiritual state of being. The Greek word "metamorphoo" which means to change from one form into another. It is where we get the English word "metamorphosis."

To give you an idea of how complete the change is, this is the word that scientists use to describe the process that turns a caterpillar into a butterfly. The other two instances of this word in the New Testament both normally translate it as "transform." Everything about this event would have been startling. The complete change, the obvious power emanating from Jesus, the meeting with Moses and Elijah, and the voice from heaven declaring the Father's love for his son, Jesus. This was a supernatural event with no other possible origin than God.

Understanding the Biblical context is difficult without certain cultural norms. All the versions share that this event began when Jesus took his closest disciples up on a mountain to pray. Then he transfigured and they saw Moses and Elijah conversing with Him. My observation leans toward the moment when Moses comes down from the mountain after receiving the ten commandments. Moses had been in such intense contact with God's presence that he was radiating light Exodus 34:29-35). Peter's response gives us a clue to this. He tells Jesus that they should build "tabernacles," one for each figure that they had seen. One of the things that Moses received instructions for in his time with God was how to build the Tabernacle, a tent for the worship of Yahweh as the Hebrew people traveled in the wilderness. Peter was just trying to respond in a way that he thought was appropriate for the moment, and his only frame of reference for an entity emanating holy light would have been the story of Moses coming down the mountain. Therefore, my story is about my life and the transformation to becoming a disciple, from a sinner to a Christian man with all the mental, and physical abuse. The failures, suffering and the tragedies of my mistakes that led to truly being transformed by the Holy Spirit. It was then Christ was the source of life itself.

Table of Contents

Chapter 1

Touched Through the Pain of Childhood

There is no doubt if you get to communicate with Gooden, his demeanor is pleasant and cheerful; he underscores this was  not always the case. Gooden grew up in Washington DC, his mother left when he was around twelve years old. He recalls that day very vividly, he exclaims. That day was the most puzzling of all days, it was because he had witnessed emotional and physical abuse in the home. Gooden's story is no stranger to the American life. Abuse is real with detrimental outcomes. He was one of the lucky ones to escape, however not without the scars. He understood the words of Charles Gordon 1971 classic play" No Place to be somebody" The dynamic of abuse in adolescence life is not often displayed the same or what you would expect. Children living in the shadow of someone else's life. Recent studies have reported that childhood abuse increased the risk of adulthood crime by promoting antisocial behavior during childhood and adolescence, followed by the formation of relationships with antisocial romantic partners and peers in adulthood. The researchers also found gender differences in the pathways linking child abuse and adult crime. Further studies suggest that stress experienced early in life damages the ability to assess risk, creating young adults with poor decision-making skills. And Since family processes and parental practices during childhood and adolescence affect whether an individual will subsequently become delinquent or criminal, it would seem to follow that adult family life might also be associated with a reduced likelihood of criminal behavior. What does it mean to live in someone's Shadow?

Gooden lived in the shadow of his father during his adolescence until he was 15 years old. His story begins.

The Lord is my shepherd; I shall not want. He makes me lie down in green pastures: he leadeth me beside the still waters. He restoreth my soul: he leadeth me in the paths of righteousness for his name's sake. Yea, though I walk through the valley of the shadow of death, I will fear no evil: for thou art with me; thy rod and thy staff they comfort me."

This I can now declare that He alone is my refuge, my place of safety; He is my God, and I am trusting him. For he rescued me from every trap and protected me from the fatal plague. He shielded me with his wings! My father owned nightclubs around the District of Columbia. I was eight when I was first introduced to the dancers which came into the club and being the boss's son, they would make a fuss all over me. It wasn't long before I developed a 'crush' on one of them. Raven was her stage name. He told his dad he wanted to go out with her so the next time she came in while he was there his dad jokingly said to her "My son thinks he's in love with you. Why don't you take him out next door for a hamburger?" So, my very first 'date' was with an older woman in my mind. I remember the scent of the atmosphere and the make-up as I sat there eating my hamburger.

Footnote: To work with polarities, you need to be able to see both perspectives clearly and at the same time. The trick isn't to solve a polarity or to make a choice and move on. Instead, you handle polarity by first recognizing what it is, and second, learning how to move mentally and practically through the ebbs and.

On another occasion at the nightclub another one of the showgirls bent down close in front of me, wearing her dance costume, (nothing) a lot of perfume, and a lot of makeup, said

14

to me in her accent "Howdy Charles Jr! You are just so cute! My name is Yum-Yum. Can I have a kiss?" (She gave him a kiss on the cheek) ......"How would you like to have a dog? I have a German Shepard called 'Pam' and unfortunately, I must give her up. Would you like her!?" What is an 8–9-year-old to do? "Sure!" I said, and a few weeks later Pam arrived. Things were bad during these times and rather traumatic, Pam had a sense of comfort that gave him an outlet, until his father took the dog and released her into Rock Creek Park. He goes on to say he does not have many good memories as a child. It was a never-ending cycle of events; and on almost every weekend I would be at my dad's bar. No place for a kid. So, all weekend I would be exposed to the sex crime and drugs which were normal occurrences. Gooden subsequently remembers the horrifying moment that began to form his opinion about life, family, and the search for happiness. He explains that his home was anything but pleasant and it didn't matter that his father was wealthy. The family was dysfunctional and lacked what it needed to form a healthy cohesiveness between the family members. It was all wrapped around a life of Sex, Drugs and Crime which were part of everyday occurrences. The exposure was unimaginable... As kids we were engrafted into a world that no child should have been exposed to. As early as ten he was cleaning his father's nightclub and learning what took place. He further explains that he could not understand what was happening to him. He had naked ladies in his face everywhere he turned. The smell of sin had a particular aroma that eventually lures you in. He did not know how to escape what had become a normal occurrence. It was during these frequent occurrences he began experimenting with alcohol, smoking and drugs as early as eleven years old. Each passing day came with a new experience in this dark hole, Gooden explains. He further remembers his first experience with cocaine. It was always just laying around with piles of money. It was easy to get drugs, therefore it became easy to begin to indulge in other drugs like angel dust, acid etc. This is when I fell into the abyss of addiction.

I was really losing control of myself; in fact, I didn't care  about anything or anyone and felt as if there was no escape. Things had gotten to a point of no return; I began craving the weekends. The dancer started paying attention to me; during the times I was behind the bar or spinning records. My father would teach me how to run the bar along with cooking and the cash register (red tape). I can vividly remember; there were always police officers at each end of the bar while I worked the bar during the night until about two and sometimes three am the next morning. The things that would take place in this three-story house connected to the nightclub were unimaginable for a kid that was only twelve years old. The atmosphere reeked the smell of sex, and drugs it felt as if flowed in every corner encapsulating its victim. This one night was a nightmare as my dad was closing in for the night, we went upstairs into the house from within the nightclub. My dad would often lock up money and drugs upstairs. While attempting to leave suddenly two men appeared with guns, wearing stocking caps over their faces. I was scared to death…I didn't know what to do. I knew I was going to die there. They tied us back-to-back in a chair. To this day, I cannot recall how my dad got loose, however he did and shot both men as they were running down the step. He had killed them both. The saga continued when the police officers came and cleaned it up like it did not happen. I was never the same after that moment. I didn't know who to be more afraid of, the cops or my dad. I would soon start using uppers and downers and purple microdot (acid) and anything I could get my hands on to take me out of this reality. I had become an addict that needed a fix and would do anything to support the habit, but ultimately the pain he was experiencing became overwhelming... So, I started stealing money from my dad. That was the easy part; there was so much money around that he wondered if his father would even know if he took it. He remembers at one point he would be so high that he would take the money get high and start ripping the money in half and tossing it in the air. This became the norm. The stealing of the money was like therapy to me. I would sometimes take the money and give it to my best friend to buy school clothes before the start of the school year. The turbulence of circumstances would only intensify. This one day I decided not to go to school, just out doing whatever. I would go home not thinking anything always tip toeing through the house. During this time, his grandmother Carrie would be there in the house to babysit because our mother was not there. She was the pillar of sanity that would be the catalyst to his life in Christ. Apparently, I had done something; or not; because if any of the other siblings got in trouble, I would be the one to pay the price for it. This one night; I recall being awoken out of my sleep; being beaten with a belt. I was distraught so I ran. So, my dad decided to tie me down to the bed, both hands and feet with my back exposed. I could hear my grandmother saying brother don't do this… my dad began beating me with an extension cord like a slave. He said with a raspy voice, "I knew I was going to die. If it had not been for my grandmother finally seeing enough; as she throws herself in the way, coming to my rescue saying you are going to kill him, otherwise he would have killed me. It was normal for him to come home drunk or under the influence and mad for no reason. This incident was unimaginable. I was never the same after that. I wanted to die. It was bad enough my mother left, and my dad was not a father but became the enemy…I began hating him. Fear was a presence that filled the house. It was the same fear I saw and felt when I was in his night clubs. He would curse and beat people just because he could… never could forget his father beating this guy who came to see my sister from down the street on Blair Road. He beat that kid all the way back home and said get your dad. He didn't want any man talking to my sister. I would slip out of the house on occasion to get away. I was terrified living in this house and so were my other siblings, especially my sister. I recall him locking me out of the house and telling the others not to let me in. During those times I would sleep across the street at Ms. Harris' home. This was my home away from the house. This became an often occurrence but on this one day as I was heading back; I discovered that my dad was trying to rape my sister. I had broken in through the basement window and upon doing so cutting my wrist just missing the main artery which needed stiches. I would solicit the help of a neighbor to get her away. The tragedy of the event would just keep happening. The women in and out as the housekeepers constantly changed, because he would throw himself on them. These events would be trailing events that ultimately threw me into a whirlwind of total chaos. The stealing of cars and breaking into his father's nightclub became a habit. I was angry! Finding in the words of Charles Gordone 1971 classic play no place to be somebody. What's happening I would constantly ask myself; and what is family love? I never knew or heard the words I love you. He further expounds about being so angry that he decided to get high and take his father's brand-new Camaro, and that his father knew he had taken the car, so he called the police and had them take him to prison, where he stayed for about two months. This was a terrifying event because he knew about prison and what happens in prison. My first day in prison was met with contention as I was going to the bathroom; a group of guys followed me in. He expounds, He could sense what was about to happen because he was considered a pretty boy. As he pauses...he says all he remembers is beating that guy so bad; they had to pull him off before the guards came. Somehow, I was able to hide during the unrest otherwise, it was going to be met with more uncertainties.

The tragedy of this all is that through my life as a kid, I

18

never got a chance to be a kid and form any childhood friendship, other than a cousin who was going through the same things that led to the discovery; that two of my cousins were raped by their dad and one possibly killed by him also, he was a cop. Gooden exhales and says his life was a tornado of unbearable events. It was like being constantly high in a dream and wishing he would just wake up. It's summer again in the night club. One of the dancers decided to show an interest in him, I'm fifteen at this point and my hormones are out of control. I didn't know what to do but she wanted to date me, but my dad got word because every woman that came to dance for him, he slept with, so this was not going to happen. She had turned him down. I was there and scared to death; this was done in the middle of the day with people in the club. She said to me come on; I'm taking you out of here. I left with her, and she took me to get my things from home later in the day to only be met with my dad lunging and swinging at me to fight me over this woman; and ultimately kicking me out the house. I was only fifteen years old when I left to stay with her in Anacostia Park, this wouldn't last long, however it provided something I had not had in a long time. Peace. Intermittently called out, as wrong as it was; it was right for that moment. I needed a place to stay. I was confused being in a relationship with this older woman and the feeling of being betrayed, lost, and forgotten. I was literally living in the darkness of sin. I felt hopeless, which only led to me dropping out of school in the eighth grade. I would often ask myself; what more could possibly happen? Nonetheless… on occasion I would hear this still calm voice of my grandmother whispering in my ear; "it's going to be alright brother". I had to find solace, all directions seemed to lead to chaos and destruction. So, I decided to take a chance; I boarded a greyhound bus to Ayden NC. to find my mother. I remember that feeling; afraid of being rejected when I arrived that night. No one came to pick me up upon my arrival, so I began walking in a strange place, the smell was different due to the country air, the trees and just being out of a concrete city. I was excited but nervous. I really needed and wanted to feel welcomed with love; instead, was met with  indifference. He said after being there for about a year and a half enrolling into school; he felt like he was just being tolerated and not really accepted or loved. So... He dropped out again and decided to go into the military at seventeen. My relationship with my mother was never felt with anything other than an acknowledgement that she is the woman that birth him but not a mother to him. My grandmother had instilled something wonderful in me through her life. I did not know at the time but despite the facts; I wouldn't disrespect her but could not find a place to put her in perspective to my life. I knew what she endured and was probably the only child that saw and heard it. A lot happened during that time, that only drove me deeper into depression. My decision to enter the military would be a great steppingstone to structure, discipline, and the ability to take instruction. I really enjoyed and appreciated the military life; however, it wasn't enough for me despite all the good things that happen during my service time before being honorably discharged in 1979, the underlined phycological scars, the pain and suffering of my childhood had a greater hold on me; and the military wasn't enough to rid me of the pain and suffering I had undergone. Then something strange started happening to me, he said. He could hear his grandmother talking to him saying..."Many are called but few are chosen, however you volunteered." Intermittently called...I did not understand this for some years. I went back to Ayden NC. I wanted to figure things out; while there, however, I discovered my military checks were being taken and cashed by my mother. I wanted to confront her but did not want to fall further, I needed to be accepted and feel loved. It wasn't enough that she left but she stole from me. I could not trust anyone. I was alone and had to find a way to cope with all the mental ills of past and present situations regarding family let alone people I did not know. So, I developed the ability to just cut people off. No attachments or trust…who could you trust if you cannot trust your own parents? I had to learn to make it on my own. I was sick and tired of being let down with the mental stresses of family. I had to find a way, but I really had no family or person to relate to about my feelings. The freedom of being employed gave a sense of direction, however escaping the abyss on my own was an impossible task along with the influence of a cousin who was into drugs, which only drove me further out of alignment with life. I thought I could control my urges…but the cocaine habit however returned with a vengeance. I recall that scripture when it said that when the devil leaves your house, he goes wondering about but comes back and finds the place he left, not kept clean, therefore coming back with more assistance, causing the second stage to be worse than the first. It's now 1980, the week of Thanksgiving. I remember that moment, the smells, and the atmosphere toxic with drugs and alcohol thus the feeling of nauseated filled my soul. On the one hand I felt we were having this amazing party; people are everywhere in the house. The excitement of feeling like you are on top of the world…however there was this intermittent touch from God that I tried to ignore... I'm so strung out that I really couldn't recognize anyone there. It was like I was in a movie. Gooden further remembers leaving the house and walking outside for a moment because of something that was taking place...his cousin was in the bathroom with a needle in his arm. Upon his return he stumbles upstairs to his room being led to get his duffle bag and stuffing it with whatever he could grab, that would fit into the bag. Gooden said he looked around, turned his back, and just walked away not knowing what to do. He called a friend to come get him…his friend said you can only stay for a couple of nights. It's Thanksgiving he recalls as he is pondering suicide. He is led to go visit his sister that ran away to Ayden NC, with tears in his eyes he recalls coming up to the door, not knowing what's inside. How will I be received again he exclaims? He loved his sister; but it had been a long time. She was the oldest but his little sister to him even though she was the oldest. He walks up to the door with this look of death, he walks in, and she takes his belonging. The atmosphere was strange; like something was inhabiting the area. I remember that moment like it was yesterday…it still brings tears to my eyes. There his sister and this elderly gentleman sitting in the corner, he had this glow…and the prettiest black and white slick hair, and a very welcoming smile on his face. He reminded him of his grandmother. He sat at the table in the corner, his sister places a plate of food on the table….and then what happens after that was something out of this world he exclaims. I was being intermittently touched in a way that I cannot explain.

Point to Ponder….

What you believe in life is in a moment in time that cannot be harnessed, however within this period life can spring up or it can cease from being. Gooden explains what happened just before he tried to eat was scary yet with a touch of peace and security beyond anything he has felt before. The only thing that ever came close to this was when he heard his grandmother's voice, it was always soft and seasoned with grace.

This intermittent touch from Christ. Gooden explains… I tried to eat but each time I raised my fork a tear would fall; it got so uncontrollable that I could not contain myself. I could hear the old gentleman saying God has something for you…he did not know God and had no idea what was happening at this point. The crying got more intense, so I fell from the table into a fetal position crying to the point of almost blanking out. Then it happened…. What happened…I did not know at the time, but the holy spirit fell upon me, and it felt as if my hands and body was plugged into an electrical socket…not painful but

22

something was happening, and it wouldn't let go. My sister was praying and said let Him fill you. I was there in that  posture for three days. Upon gathering myself and trying to understand what happened…I was told…that I was being filled with something that he knew nothing about. I heard myself speaking in another tongue and I could not control it during this interaction, it was like I was having an out of body experience. The most amazing aspect of this encounter was that after coming out of it; I felt like I was brand new. The peace and calm about myself and the desire for drugs and alcohol was gone. Yes gone!!! Gooden further says it was several days later when he began remembering what had taken place. His sister gave him temporary lodging. He got a job working with this housing authority. Then something amazing would take place for three years. Gooden explains. I had this earnest desire to know God through Christ, so for three years I would walk the railroad track in this small town of Ayden North Carolina, talking to God every night reading the bible and asking question. The interesting aspect of this encounter was the more I read and talked to God the more I would understand the bible and the more Christ would be revealed. Stop for a moment. I know this may sound unreal to many of you. However, have you really gotten to that point where you totally surrendered to Christ? Gooden further say the desire for drugs, alcohol, sex, and anything that was associated with his life before Christ had been wiped away thrown in that sea of forgetfulness. Gooden further suggest that these intermittent initial touches where critical in his first three-year journey as a new Christian. He had no idea on how to talk to God, so he talked the only way he knew. Gooden stops again to say that as a child he was very shy and had a stammering tongue like Moses, God touched my tongue. He further elaborates because of the drugs especially the angle dust, his ability to think clearly was somewhat handicap. My sister gave me my first bible in 1980, that I still have today. I went through every page of this book. Christ through His holy spirit began to teach me the scriptures and its interpretation. I devoted myself to doing nothing but work and studying. This would go on for three years. What happened in those three years was insurmountable; Gooden explains. The word came alive and started manifesting itself in unexplainable ways. I had a question that needed to be answered, I had problems that I could not understand. I had pain and suffering from people and circumstance, yet the focus was to understand Christ before understanding the why to my life. The following are a few examples that were very relatable to me understanding the why in my season as I was transitioning through life: Gideon and Joseph experience along with Paul on the road to Damascus. I heard God calling me in the middle of the night to go proclaim the gospel message. I proclaimed the first message September 1984 with the United Pentecostal Church which ordained me as an evangelist. This would be just the beginning of intermittent touches through the holy spirit. The revelation I accepted forewarned me that this new life would not exempt me from more events over the life span of my existence next forty-three years; however, each day would reveal to him what he continues to search for...the wisdom to understand the daily vises and to overcome each day in the day because there is no other way. As I was maturing after years of trials and tribulations, I realized I like to write so I began telling myself stories and just cataloging them. I had a gift to communicate and teach So, with no prior training I started writing and holding large and small groups meeting in the parks around Pitt County, telling people about the wisdom of God outside of their religious biases. Gooden's writings are a compilation of years of submitting, failing, divorce, rejection, suicide, betrayal, racial discrimination, religious discrimination, abandonment, being alone and discovering himself each day was a challenge and remains one with a new desire to serve Christ more each day. Enjoy the wisdom of

"When A Man Is Intermittently Touched by God."

Gooden further states he would be remis if he didn't acknowledge that divorce was the greatest catalyst to his intermittent touch from God. It wasn't that God wanted it to happen, it was his own choices that allowed it to happen. However, outside the will of God and making choices based on fleshly desire will always inhibit the presence of Christ and you will always get the results of your own action. We can get out of the will of God as a believer, but you can get back up again. The truth of the matter is most of life decision were a result of my past and most of my journey after were a result of my decision and not allowing the word of God to transform me. Or perhaps…maybe this was my journey? I must admit I was not ready…I was saved but had too much unresolved pain that I just thought was going to go away without acknowledgment. I had to finally realize God did not make us island off alone but called us one body in Christ. I was not ready, nor was it the season, and neither were the other people. I was just tired of being and feeling alone and carrying a lot of baggage. This caused endless pain for himself, his children and all involved. Gooden states you can never take back what has been done, you can only move forward in the moment and accept the truth at the starting line of the new day. It's the only place in time you can rest. What has been spent is gone. God forgives so forgive yourself even if others do not. You are not responsible for others; you are responsible for what you do to others...

Chapter 2

Touched in My Betrayal

How does anyone begin to explain being betrayed; it's painful no matter which end of the spectrum you may find  yourself on. The pain is the same regardless. Gooden understands betrayal as one of the most painful human experiences. The discovery that someone we trusted has pulled the reality rug from under us. Gooden further exclaims dealing with the betrayal of the woman that gave him life was the most painful. He had to witness his birth mother leaving one early evening just before the sun was about to set. She leaves with her suitcase, as he is seated at the top step of their porch on Delafield place. It was three flights of stairs she had to walk down; for sure he thought, she had time to change her mind. However, he remembers the walk as he sat there crying in bewilderment. Why…with no answer just a walk to this white car to never return. He was left there with his sister and three other siblings, the youngest was still a baby. It was bad enough that the family had lost two other children. What could have been going on in her heart and mind? How would we be taken care of? What would be the outcome of our lives? The cause and effect of those decisions in the circle of influence will undoubtably become our fate regardless of who is at the helm.

How do you even begin to ascertain what is happening at any point and time when one feels betrayed? Gooden suggests that feeling although has the same result as pain, however each person reflects on experiences differently. Gooden continues. The betrayal of his father only made matters worse. The attention that each sibling needed during this time was almost impossible to obtain. Although his father provided food, clothing, and shelter; the necessities of life, it was not coupled with love, understanding or care. As a matter of fact, it was anything but love. We were afraid to do anything, in fear of just being beaten and or beaten in our sleep. Our grandmother who was the staple would try her best, but we even saw her being betrayed by her own son. To the point that he slammed her arm in a swinging door. She would only say…" That's alright brother." When we see the word "betrayal" we may immediately think "affair." But betrayal comes in many forms. Abandonment, vicious gossip, and spreading lies also may be experienced as betrayal. The damaging aspect of betrayal is that our sense of reality is undermined. What felt like solid trust suddenly crumbles. Our innocence is shattered, we're left wondering what happened; how could this happen and who is this person? It's one thing to get it from immediate family, but to get it from the circle of influence within relatives, friends co-workers also affect our conscious awareness of the associated pain which is equally detrimental. To be told you aren't going to be anything. Gooden says these were words that triggered his emotional stressors, hence why he felt so inadequate. It wasn't that he couldn't learn as a young child, there just wasn't any positive reinforcement in the home. Some betrayals leave us with little choice but to heal and move on with our lives, such as when we're suddenly abandoned. Some betrayals leave us so confused that we find ourselves in the words of Charles Gordone 1971 classic play "No Place to be Somebody." Affairs are more complex. Should we gather our dignity and end the relationship? Or is there a way to maintain our dignity while attempting to heal and rebuild trust?

What does betrayal do to a person?

Betrayal is serious because it destroys trust, and without trust relationships, social circles, families, institutions and most certainly a marriage cannot function. For example...Jesus understood the polarity of differences in the paradox of betrayal during a pivotal point in His life… He understands and knows that Judas is about to betray Him, He also knows that Peter is going to deny Him, not once but three times. How do you think He must have felt? The Bible teaches betrayal is always the result when we refuse God's will and fight for our own. To be a disciple who endures mean your desire is not to betray God, our spouse, and those we love. We must be disciples who submit to the will of God. Perhaps love is still alive, and our partner admits his or her mistake and expresses remorse. Betrayal has a choice and must ask the question. Would it be a courageous risk to give our partner another chance or a foolish mistake to trust again? Rather than act impulsively, we may serve ourselves by taking time to sort out our feelings and find some clarity about what's best for us. Subsequentially, it is better to put your trust in God than your confidence in man. Hence that means yourself also… Betrayals are founded on two building blocks: deception (not revealing your true needs to avoid conflict) and a yearning for emotional connection from outside the relationship. Matthew 7:12 So, in everything, do to others what you would have them do to you, for this sums up the Law and the Prophets. Gooden suggest, it takes courage to consider whether we might have played some unknowing role in a betrayal. Maybe we neglected someone including oneself in some subtle way. By breaking or violating a presumptive contract, trust, or confidence produces moral and psychological conflict within all relationships. Gooden also put emphasis on the betrayal of the Church, which has crumbled the innocence and shattered our community of the foundational building blocks of truth with deception for mere gain.

Chapter 3

Intermittent Forgiveness

As Christians, it is our goal to be led of the Spirit and not operate in the flesh. However, Gooden explains that it is easier said  than done when we aren't abiding close to the cross. We will have times of testing and moments when we will miss the mark. As a matter of fact. The scripture implies that a righteous man falls seven times but gets back up. Forgiveness is always the leading of the Holy Spirit. God is quick to forgive. Gooden further communicates it was very hard to trust let alone forgive people. Therefore, the pain that was bottled up inside, became the very thing that would enslave him and inhibit him from making sound decision in his early years as a Christian. He hadn't realized the pain of unforgiveness he was experiencing. It took years of repeating the same things and expecting a different result to finally get a glimpse of being free. Then one day the holy spirit revealed his heart unto him. The greatest pain he had to overcome was with his parents and to forgive himself. He felt abandoned and alone most of his life. Then early in the am one morning, being led by the spirit, he threw some clothes on, jumped in the car, and drove to Washington, D.C to visit his father's grave. He exclaimed he had no idea where the grave was, so he called his youngest brother to get directions. It was dead of winter and freezing cold, and it started to snow Gooden communicates. I started to turn around but kept going. This trip was a precursor to several of event that resulted in the healing and peace of God that would ultimately free him from the chains that was holding him down.

Gooden goes on to say, this event was like the event he had when he was filled with the spirit of Christ. Upon arrival at the grave all I could do was cry, when I got to the grave, he cried more uncontrollably. It was there he fell to his knees and thanked his dad for the life he had given him. The understanding of the polarity of difference in this paradox of abuse was and wasn't about what had happened to him as a child, it was what he was going to do as an adult. He gave me what he had to give. He now had to release the past and forgive, to be set free from unforgiveness. This also had to happen with his mother. It was at this junction that another touch by Christ would enter his life.

"For Thou, Lord, art good, and ready to forgive; and plenteous in mercy unto all of them that call upon Thee" (Psalm 86:5 KJV).

Forgiveness is the key to becoming one.

"And so, He condemned sin in sinful man, in order that the righteous requirements of the law might be fully met in us who do not live according to the sinful nature but live according to the Spirit. Those who live according to the sinful nature (flesh) have their minds set on what that nature desires; but those who live in accordance with the Spirit have their minds set on what the Spirit desires. The mind of sinful man is death, but the mind controlled by the Spirit is life and peace because the sinful mind (flesh) is hostile to God. It does not submit to God, nor can it do so" (Romans 8:3-7 NIV).

Touched to Believe and Forgive.

The word of God shows us that undealt frustrations lead to betrayal (John 12:3-6, Matthew 26:14-16). Those who proclaim Christ for a period only to turn away later do so through a process. When we don't deal with frustrations in our walk with God, our marriage, and other relationships, they allow bitterness to creep in and sets the stage for a betrayal. Judas did not like some of the things Jesus did, like how Jesus viewed and used money. As this frustration grew, Judas became more and more willing to betray Jesus. We will never fully know the true motives in Judas' heart during those moments of betrayal. But what is interesting is that during that period, 30 pieces of silver was not a vast sum of money. So, to me, it seems more likely that Judas did not betray Jesus out of greed but out of bitterness. Perhaps Judas, like many of us chose to overlook what his intention were about when the Pharisees suggested this price, the price of a common slave. It seems Judas' anger and frustration had grown over these three years of ministry together. He was fed up with his expectations of Jesus constantly not being unmet. Jesus had wasted one too many dollars, He rebuked Judas one too many times, Judas was tired of being listed last every time, he was tired of the religious leaders shaking their heads at him as he followed this crazy leader called Jesus. And so, Judas betrayed Jesus with a cold, calculated slap in the face. He could have just pointed Him out; instead, his actions represented what was in his heart. How did Judas grow so bitter? How did he become so blinded by his disgust with Jesus? Like many of us, undealt with frustrations eventually always boil over. In any relationship, pretending there isn't a problem is a prerequisite for a betrayal. Affairs don't just happen. A teenager leaving one day and never calling his parents again isn't because of a singular event. Best friends don't split because of one argument. People betray one another once the frustrations are too much to handle because they were never dealt with properly. As Ephesians 4:26-27 states, "Do not let the sun go down while you are still angry, and do not give the devil a foothold." Like any man who eventually betrays someone, Judas couldn't take it anymore. He had kept his mouth shut long enough. Since he never dealt with his frustrations and confusions properly, now he was going to do something about it, no matter how sinful it was. Judas let it get so bad that he eventually betrayed Jesus to death because Judas was in denial about his sin.

Peter dealt with the same frustration as Judas. He had to accept his over zealousness which led to his own denial of Jesus Christ. He is one of the most fascinating figures in the New Testament. A prominent early-church figure. There's a lot of emphasis on Peter's penchant for hasty, reckless behavior, but the fact that he plays such a notable role in the Gospels helps account for many of those shortcomings. We're not given as much insight into the other disciples' personalities, so we're going to focus on Peter. However, Peter's denial of Jesus is one particularly heartbreaking moment featured in all four of the Gospels. As readers, we see Jesus warn Peter that this moment is coming; we watch the denial happen and witness Peter's immediate heartbreak, realizing what he'd done. We also get a front-row seat to his restoration. Can you imagine them disputing over whose to be the greatest. Jesus said to them, "The kings of the Gentiles lord it over them; and those who exercise authority over them call themselves Benefactors. But you are not to be like that. Instead, the greatest among you should be like the youngest, and the one who rules like the one who serves. For who is greater, the one who is at the table or the one who serves? Is it not the one who is at the table? But I am among you as one who serves. You are one of those who have stood by me in my trials. And I confer on you a kingdom, just as my Father conferred one on me, so that you may eat and drink at my table in my kingdom and sit on thrones, judging the twelve tribes of Israel. It is here we must stop and recognize that it was during these times and moments the spirit intermittently orchestrates events. The tailwind of the event shows itself. Listen to the words of Christ.

"Simon, Simon, Satan has asked to sift all of you as wheat. But I have prayed for you, Simon, that your faith may not fail. And when you have turned back, strengthen your brothers. "But he replied, "Lord, I am ready to go with you to prison and to death." Jesus answered, "I tell you, Peter, before the rooster crows today, you will deny me three times that you know me" (Luke 22:24–34). Jesus reiterates a point He made when frustration erupted among the disciples because James and John had requested prominent positions in Jesus' coming kingdom (Matthew 20:20–28). The greatest are those that serve. Jesus came as one who serves; if we genuinely want to be like Him, we'll also serve. Jesus then turns His attention to Peter, and it's hard to know just how this shift occurs. It might be that Peter made a forceful case that he was the greatest of the apostles. But Jesus alerts Peter that a moment of trial is coming for them all. It's touching that Jesus also lets Peter know He's been praying for the disciple. It's a good reminder for all of us of the words of Paul: who then is the one who condemns? No one. Christ Jesus who died more than that, who was raised to life, is at the right hand of God and is also interceding for us (Romans 8:34).

After hearing Jesus' warning, Peter informs the Lord that he's courageous and ready to die if he must. Jesus responds by getting very specific, letting Peter know he'll deny the Lord three times today. John's account of the evening dramatically cuts back and forth between Jesus' trial and Peter's experience in the courtyard. The other disciple, who was known to the high priest, came back, spoke to the servant girl on duty there and brought Peter in.

"You are one of this man's disciples too, aren't you?" she asked Peter. He replied, "I am not."

It was cold, and the servants and officials stood around a fire they had made to keep warm. Peter also was standing with them, warming himself (John 18:15–18). After Peter's first denial, John switches the narrative to Jesus before the high priest (John 18:19–24), brilliantly comparing Jesus' response to His interrogation with Peter's. As accusations are leveled against Jesus, He refuses to deny the charges. Peter, on the other hand, denies everything. Meanwhile, Simon Peter was still standing there warming himself. So, they asked him, "You are one of his disciples too, aren't you?" He denied it, saying, "I am not."

WHAT WILL YOU CHOOSE

You're hanging in the balance of heaven and hell.
Captured now by Satan's spell.
Many doors that you might choose.
Take the wrong one, and your soul!
You'll lose.
It's not a game that Satan plays,
As he draws your mind into a maze.
It's true that the wages of sin is death
and hell, a reality not just a myth.
Choose this day whom you will serve.
Let Jesus Christ your soul preserve.
How could you trade his priceless treasure
For just a few moments of fleeting pleasure?
Life here is short, oh why can't you see.
It's nothing compared to eternity.
Look up, reach out and take Gods hand!
And he'll lead you safely to the promised land.
A snare for your soul, did the enemy weave.
But you can be set free,
Only trust and believe.

Chapter 4

Intermittent Restoration...Peter

Jesus appears to the disciples more than once, and Peter is present, but Peter had to feel that his denial was hanging over the joy of Jesus' resurrection and the connection the two had previously shared. When the moment presents itself, Jesus finally addresses the topic. When they had finished eating, Jesus said to Simon Peter, "Simon son of John, do you love me more than these?" "Yes, Lord," he said, "you know that I love you. "Jesus said, "Feed my lambs. "Again, Jesus said, "Simon son of John, do you love me?" He answered, "Yes, Lord, you know that I love you. "Jesus said, "Take care of my sheep." The third time he said to him, "Simon son of John, do you love me?" Peter was hurt because Jesus asked him the third time, "Do you love me?" He said, "Lord, you know all things; you know that I love you." Jesus said, "Feed my sheep. Very truly I tell you, when you were younger you dressed yourself and went where you wanted; but when you are old you will stretch out your hands, and someone else will dress you and lead you where you do not want to go." Jesus said this to indicate the kind of death by which Peter would glorify God. Then he said to him, "Follow me" (John 21:15–19)!

Jesus asks him, "Do you love me more than these?" Peter has often been vocal about his faithfulness, suggesting that even if others fall away, he never would (Matthew 26:33), that he would be willing to lay down his life for Jesus (John 13:37), and promising to go to prison or die for Jesus (Luke 22:33). Considering Peter's denial, Jesus pointedly asks him if he still considers himself the most faithful disciple. Peter is forced to consider the rashness of previous commitments. Three times the Lord asks if Peter loves Him, and each time Peter affirms that he does. Each time Jesus instructs the disciple to demonstrate that love by serving each other. Jesus then explains to Peter that he is, in fact, going to suffer for following Him. And after all this, Jesus issued the same invitation that He gave Peter at the beginning, "Follow me."

What can we learn from Peter's denial of Jesus?

Gooden finally understood like Peter that words spoken in the heat of the moment do not always hold water. Like Peter, it's easy for us to believe that we're more faithful and courageous than we truly are. However, it isn't until we encounter difficult and challenging moments that we discover the truth to who we are. Sometimes those moments reveal sinful and broken areas we have yet to identify and deal with. Consider this, when we fail, there's a huge temptation to give up. Many people have made tragic decisions, and the shame of those decisions caused them to walk away from Christian community. But it's important to remember that failure isn't fatal. Jesus is concerned about redemption, and not allowing failure to be your last words in life.

As He did with Peter, Jesus wants to heal us, restore us, and invite us to recommit following Him. And when we let Him, we might discover that our intermittent experiences good and bad have made us stronger, wiser, and more compassionate than we would have been otherwise.

Men Touched by God

The Bible is full of examples of men who enjoyed an intermittent intimate relationship with the Almighty. Noah, Abraham, Moses, David, and Elijah are just a few examples. Each one had different characteristics that earned him the title "man of faith", but they all shared one commonality – they walked with God.

What does it mean to walk with God? It means to have a close relationship with Him whereby we obey His commands and follow His ways along with trusting Him during the adversarial moments. It's not just a one-time event but rather a lifestyle. It's living our lives in such a way that pleases Him.

Walking with God has its rewards. One of them is eternal life. However, the cross comes with a burden also. When we walk with God, we are promised a place in His eternal kingdom. We also become temples of the Living God and His Spirit dwells within us. And as His children, we have access to the blood of Jesus that washes away our sins and gives us new life.

So let us strive to be men who walk with God, close enough to hear Him when He speaks, by allowing the intermittent experiences move you towards the following:

- Being led by the Holy Spirit
- Living righteously.
- Walking by faith; allowing scriptures to lead.
- Having a healthy respect for Him
- Close fellowship with other believers
- Allowing what you do to please Christ and not men.
- Studying to show yourself approved unto God.
- Displaying reverence for who He is.
- Divine relationship, with the ability, to fall before Him when you fail Him.

Matthew 8:1-3 if you were ever to visit Rome, your trip would include a tour of the Sistine Chapel, which has the same measurements as Solomon's Temple in the Old Testament: 134 feet long and forty-four feet wide. You would walk in and immediately be awed by the masterpieces of art that were painted directly on the walls about five hundred years ago. You would walk out into the very center of the room, and when you looked up, you would be stunned by Michelangelo's masterpieces painted on the ceiling, 68 feet above the floor. You would see nine different scenes from the Book of Genesis—and right in the middle of the ceiling, you would see what has been called "The Creation of Adam." It is one of the most widely recognized scenes in the history of art. Its" the one where God is reaching out His hand to Adam, their fingers nearly touching. The Bible tells us that God breathed into Adam, and he became a living being. But that is just the way that Michelangelo depicted God creating life into the body of Adam. Imagine what that must have been like! If God touched, you with his finger of love!

I was intermittently touched by Him." But I want to tell you today that our being touched by God has nothing to do with our talent, our brains, or earthly wisdom. All of us can be touched by the Almighty Hand of God—and it can happen today and as a matter-of-fact God intermittently gives every man a measure of faith. In Matthew 8:1-3 we have read about a man whom Jesus touched and healed of his leprosy. But that is only one place we can read about the touch of God upon our lives. We see touching throughout the Scriptures. It conveys love, understanding, healing, and life in Christ. It speaks when words cannot be used. But what happens when God touches our lives?

When God touches us, we are declared Not Guilty! Isaiah sixth chapter talks about a vision he had one day, in which he saw the Lord God sitting on His throne. When he recognized the holiness of God, Isaiah saw how unclean he himself was. One of the attendants around the throne came to Isaiah with a burning coal, touched his lips, and said, "Now you are pronounced Not guilty". Your sins are all forgiven. You and I can experience the same sort of cleansing in our lives today. When God touches our lips, or our minds, or our hearts, with the burning coal and convicting power of His Holy Spirit, we are declared, not guilty. We realize now that Jesus loves us and takes our shattered lives into His tender, understanding hands. He forgives us and forgets the past with all its failures, and the sins that have kept us from walking each day with Him. Psalm 103:12 declares a living reality for us: As far as the east is from the west, so far has He removed our transgressions from us.

Gooden reminisces, he wasn't supposed to make it let alone be here today. He was smoking angel dust which pretty much destroys your brain. But ...the power of God restores all things. Our own minds and hearts might continue to dredge things up to the surface, things that have been buried for a long, long time. I had a lot of scares and pain, however just because we can remember them and feel badly about them doesn't mean that God hasn't forgiven us! When our lives are really, really touched by God, we are declared "Not guilty" and all those things in our past are gone forever. Jesus has paid the penalty for our sins once for all.

Chapter 5

Touched by a New life

On this one special occasion, Jesus entered local Jewish synagogue. Then a rabbi said, "My little daughter has just  died, but you can bring her back to life again if you will only come and touch her. "So, Jesus went back to the home of the rabbi, where the noisy mourning crowds were. He said, "Get them out, for the little girl isn't dead; she's only sleeping." The Bible says that everyone there scoffed and sneered at Him. God touched her, and she was given new life! Sometimes we think that a person is so low in sin, that they're beyond hope. Sometimes we might even think that about ourselves; I certainly did. But that's not what the Bible declares. The scripture declares that we who were once dead in sin, have been given new life in Christ! Listen to this: Anyone who has died has been freed from sin. Now if we have died with Christ, we believe that we will also live with him. For we know that since Christ was raised from the dead, He cannot die again; death no longer has mastery over Him. The death He died, He died to sin once for all; but the life He lives, He lives to God. In the same way, count yourselves dead to sin but alive to God in Christ Jesus. (Romans 6:7-11). I had developed a reliance on substances that would prevent me from logical thinking. Which rocket into displaced decision and a reckless life. When your life is touched by God, that is the beginning of a new, abundant life! After Jesus raised the little daughter of the Rabbi, two blind men followed along behind Jesus. They began shouting, "O Son of David, have mercy on us." When they followed Jesus into the house where He was staying, Jesus asked them, "Do you believe I can make you see?" They told Him, "Yes, Lord."

The Bible reads that then Jesus touched their eyes, and told them, "Because of your faith, it will happen." And suddenly they could see! After we are given new life in Christ, our spiritual eyes can see, to understand, to discern the things of the Spirit of God. This is exactly what happened to me, the scriptures cannot lie.

Paul wrote in 1 Corinthians 1:18, "I know very well how foolish it sounds to those who are lost, when they hear that Jesus died to save them. But we who are saved recognize this message as the very power of God. "And in the second chapter: But the man who isn't a Christian can't understand and can't accept these thoughts from God, which the Holy Spirit teaches us. They sound foolish to him, because only those who have the Holy Spirit within them can understand what the Holy Spirit means. Those of us who are Christians today can understand what Paul was talking about. You can understand the things of the Spirit of God. You can understand what Jesus did to save us from our sins, to give us new life. You can understand how the Holy Spirit works in our lives to reprove, to convict, to consecrate. However, when I was in darkness, I could not understand those things that should have had meaning let alone understanding. I once was blind, but now I see! When we are touched by God, God speaks through us. In the first chapter of Jeremiah, we see that the Lord said to Jeremiah, "Before you were born, I sanctified you and appointed you as My spokesman to the world." Jeremiah's answer sounds like a lot of people I've known when they have been asked to do something. Jerimiah said, "O Lord God, I can't do that!" But listen to the rest of his answer: "I'm far too young! I am only a youth!" God replied, "Do not say that, for you will go wherever I send you and speak whatever I tell you. And don't be afraid of the people, for I, the Lord, will be with you and see you through. "Then God touched Jeremiah's mouth and said, "See, I have put My words in your mouth!" When we are touched by God, and when we have fully dedicated ourselves to Christ, and when we have been truly born again, then God is going to put His words into our mouths, so that we may speak for Him. I am not saying that every Christian should preach, or teach or sing, but every Christian does have opportunities every day when we can speak on behalf of Jesus Christ. When God touches your life, He frees you from all your hang-ups and fears that have kept your voice silent. When God touches our lives, we intermittently develop an insight into our own inabilities.

I had those fears, with failed relationships, and people not understanding me, and living to please people because you just want to be a part of something. In most cases you are not helping yourself but inhibiting the plan of God in your life. It is not about acceptance in the world but acceptance in Christ. God speak through us. You cannot know the forgiveness of Christ until you have been declared not guilty. You cannot be set free from the deadness of sin until you accept the new life Christ offers to you. You cannot receive and understand the voice of the spirit speaking to you until God touches your life; that's when He will begin to speak through you with clear and decisive understanding with clarity. Have you ever been outside playing, and your mother called you, what was that like when you knew by her tone, she was looking for you? Over and over and over God calls for you to come to Him, to allow Him to touch your life, to forgive you of your sins, to cleanse your life, to give your life insight which enables you the privilege of sharing Him with others. Do you dare to say to Him, "Do you want me, God, or are you only just doing your own thing"? "Yes, He wants you. Even now, and every second of your life, He reaches out to touch you—like Michelangelo's painting of God reaching toward Adam. Will you reach out to Him? If by faith you reach out to Him, He will meet your every need. He will respond to the cry of your heart. He will touch you and set you free. Rise and be healed in the name of Jesus. Let faith arise in the light of your new life. But realize the men who walked with God, or walked with Jesus avoided things like ungodly sinners, the desires of the flesh, and the wickedness of man. The Bible is full of examples of men who enjoyed an intimate relationship with the Almighty. Noah, Abraham, Moses, David, and Elijah are just a few examples. Each one had distinctive characteristics that earned him the title "man of faith," but they all shared one commonality – they avoided people who did not obey the laws of God; they avoided anything that would lead them astray from God; they avoided ungodly acts, like murder, adultery, stealing, and lying. These men wanted to be far away from anything that could potentially ruin their relationship with Him.

So, let us all strive to be men who walk with God. Close enough to hear Him when He speaks and not ahead of His guidance. There are many men who have walked with God throughout the Bible and history that have fallen, however it was intermittent. They are examples to us of how to live close to God and please Him. By following their examples, we can learn how to walk with God ourselves.

Touch me God

Daniel testified, "Behold, a hand touched me, which set me upon my knees and upon the palms of my hands" (Daniel

10:10). The word for "touched" here means to "violently seize upon." Daniel was saying, in essence, "When God placed his hand on me, it put me on my face. His touch gave me an urgency to pray, to seek him with all that's in me." This happens anytime God touches someone's life. That person falls to his knees and becomes a man of prayer, driven to seek the Lord. I stopped wondering why he touches only certain people with this urgency. God-touched servants that wanted an intimate relationship with the Lord, receiving revelations from heaven and enjoying a walk with Christ that few others do. Why are some hungry seekers while others go their own way? I believe Daniel was a devoted servant touched by God in a supernatural way. There were many other good, pious people serving the Lord on Daniel's day: Shadrach, Meshach, and Abednego, as well as other Israelites who maintained their faith as well while enslaved in Babylon. So, why did God intermittently lay his hand on Daniel and touch him as he did? Why was this one man able to see and hear things no one else could? He declares, "I Daniel alone saw the vision: for the men that were with me saw not the vision" (10:7). Here was the incredible vision Daniel saw: "In the four and twentieth day of the first month, as I was by the side of the great river…I lifted up mine eyes, and looked, and behold a certain man clothed in linen, whose loins were girded with fine gold…His body also was like the beryl, and his face as the appearance of lightning, and his eyes as lamps of fire, and his arms and feet like in color to polished brass" (10:4-6). This was a vision of Christ himself, clear and vivid. In fact, it was the same vision given to John on the Isle of Patmos (see Revelation 1:13-15). Now God spoke to Daniel unmistakably, "like the voice of a multitude" (Daniel 10:6). This wasn't a peep or a whisper, but the thunderous sound of a roaring tumult. The Lord revealed himself to Daniel this way for a specific reason: He wanted to end the long famine of his Word. He decided the time had come to deliver a message to lost humanity. And He wanted his servants to know what he was about to do and why: "To make thee understand what shall befall thy people in the latter days" (10:14). But God needed a voice to speak his message. He wanted a praying servant, someone who would respond faithfully to His calling. Daniel was that man. He'd been praying devoutly three times a day. Now, as he walked along the river, Christ revealed himself to him and Daniel was shattered by the experience. He says, "A great quaking fell upon them, so that they fled to hide themselves. Therefore, I was left alone, and saw this great vision, and there remained no strength in me…Yet I heard the voice of his words" (10:7-9). Scripture doesn't identify the men who were with Daniel. They might have been Babylonian guards or government officials. After all, Daniel occupied a high office in the kingdom. In my opinion, these men were Israelites, specifically Daniel's pious friends and associates. Yet, if that's so, why did they flee? Daniel says they saw and heard nothing. Why would they be compelled to hide?

Here is why: God was purposefully preparing Daniel. He was preparing his servant, body, and soul, to receive a word from heaven. Whenever God touches one of his praying servants, He manifests himself in that human vessel. First, He intermittently strips him of all self, and then He totally prepares him. The sight of this process can strike fear in flesh-bound Christians. It either causes their hidden sin to melt, or it prompts them to flee the scene. I remember such a stirring in my own life, several years ago, after divorce. I was sitting on the patio. Suddenly, God's Spirit gripped me, and I fell on my face. I was distraught and confused. My question to God was Why? The Lord began to speak to my heart about my lost soul. And that I needed to go back and do the first work…Sound familiar? Soon I was weeping and prophesying over my own life. I felt as if I were in God's very presence, removed from this world. His Spirit was moving on me, calling me, giving me a vision for ministry. I do not know how long I was in that state. All I know is, during this time I knew what I had to do. I've often wondered about the touch of God simply a matter of predestination. Are those who receive his touch chosen and elected for it before they're even born? Is it merely their destiny to be dedicated to prayer, filled by the Holy Spirit, given words from God? I ask these questions because of an unexplainable, God-given hunger in my soul. My inner man yearns for a revelation of Christ. Something in me simply won't settle for another person's revelation. Why? I'm convinced God has a particular word He wants to speak to this generation. And right now, He's searching the earth for servants He can fill with His Holy Spirit. He wants men who'll serve as His oracles to a lost world. Only His powerful, anointed word can combat the rising spirit of our adversary the devil and false prophets, it is only His truth that can deal a deathblow to the self-interest, materialism, and lust in his own church.

A pure word is about to come forth in the earth once more. Convicting truth will be taught/preached from the lips of a new generation of God's people who have set their hearts on Christ. Even now the Lord is raising up men who are touched and filled with the Holy Spirit. He's going to set these servants on fire with His truth. His touch on their lives will cause the whole world to take notice.

God Touches a Man

When Christ calls a man, He bids him come and intermittently die. "The cross is laid on every Christian. The first call which every man must experience is the call to abandon the attachments of this world. It is that dying of the  old man which is the result of Gooden's encounter with Christ. The cross is laid on every human's foot to accept. As we embark upon discipleship, we must surrender ourselves to Christ in union with His death, burial, and resurrection. We must submit our lives to death. Thus, it begins, the new life of a believer to the cross. This life will be met with difficulties, Gooden explains. However, is not the end, but the beginning of the intermittent submission for a life of peace and joy in Christ.

When Christ (kaleo) calls a man, He bids him come and die. It may be a death like that of the first disciples who had to leave what they knew and follow a man who they knew nothing of. Christ the natural man had to overcome the same physical death we must commit to reign with Him.

The Purpose of Living Righteously

A righteous man does not look to the left or right from doing what God has defined as right. He is ruled by God's foundational unchangeable principles and not the tradition of men or the world.

There are three important elements to living righteously.

Hearing

- "How shall they believe in Him whom they have not heard? And how shall they hear without a preacher? This is the process where God communicates to man what he is expected to do. The conscience is very limited and not at all perfect, but it is one means God communicates His standard of righteousness with us. God also uses preachers to pass on His word and the gospel.

Knowing

- "How then shall they call upon Him in whom they have not believed?" Knowledge of God's ways alone never saves. Knowledge leads to pride. Think of the Sadducees. Their name has its origins in the Hebrew root word for righteousness. They claimed to live righteous lives, but they manipulated God's standard and was often rebuked by Jesus. We must accept God's ways in our belief, and our faith.

- Obedience is when we take God's Word and live it out consistently in our lives.

Gooden contains that until we recognize the sovereignty of Christ in God through the Holy spirit it will be impossible for anyone to comprehend, let alone understand the mysteries of God in the bible. He uses the foolish things of this world to confound the wisdom of this world.

MY CHILD

Black child, you're my treasure lost.
I seek to find you at all costs.
I've sent my people out to search for your soul,
To make you my bride and make you whole.
So, when you hear my call,
Don't run but yield to the pleas of the Holy one.
For it was for you I have suffered and died.
If only you could see the tears I've cried,
You'd know of the love, with which I woo,
If you would allow me to sup with you.
I know what it takes to make you happy and free,
And all your treasures can be found in me!

Chapter 6

Never Stop Seeking

God made Daniel his oracle because he never let up in prayer. The Lord touches every servant who is faithful in  prayer. He seeks out those who are willing to discipline themselves to hear His voice. The Bible calls this attitude "setting the heart." Daniel writes, "I (intermittently) set my face unto the Lord God, to seek by prayer and supplications, with fasting, and sackcloth, and ashes" (Daniel 9:3). Daniel then tells us, "Whiles I was speaking, and praying, and confessing my sin and the sin of my people Israel and presenting my supplication before the Lord my God...the man Gabriel, whom I had seen in the vision at the beginning, being caused to fly swiftly, touched me about the time of the evening oblation" (Daniel 9:20-21). In short, Daniel is saying, "God touched me while I was seeking him in intense prayer." Daniel makes it clear: He didn't get his understanding of God's Word by studying under learned men. He didn't gain his knowledge of future events from Babylon's institutions. Nobody could teach him how to interpret dreams that were supernaturally given. Daniel declares, "Whiles I was speaking in prayer...He informed me...and said, O Daniel, I am now come forth to give thee skill and understanding" (9:21-22). Simply put, Daniel's prayers brought forth a Word from God's throne. "Then he said unto me, Fear not, Daniel: for from the first day that thou didst set thine heart to understand, and to chasten thyself before thy God, thy words were heard, and I am come for thy words...Now I am come to make thee understand what shall befall thy people in the latter days" (10:12,14).

Point to Ponder….

It wasn't until I started to die to what people thought and their direction for my life that my life took on a different path. I wasn't to get the approval of men but walk in the direction of the Holy Spirit.

What kind of praying had Daniel been doing to prompt such a visitation? Scripture tells us he'd spent three weeks in utter brokenness: "In those days Daniel was mourning three full weeks. He ate no pleasant bread, neither came flesh nor wine in his mouth, neither did he anoint himself at all, till three whole weeks were fulfilled" (10:2-3). Daniel had spent twenty-one days humbling himself, mourning on his knees, chastening his flesh, setting his heart to receive divine understanding. He was making a declaration of war: "Lord, I won't leave your presence until I discern what you're doing. I don't care what cost I must pay. "Something else happened to Daniel while he prayed. He was brought to the end of his fleshly speaking abilities. The Lord now touched Daniel's lips so he could speak as his oracle. He told his servant, "I have sanctified your tongue. Now I'm going to speak through you. Anyone who speaks for God must have his tongue purged and purified. It happened with Isaiah and Jeremiah. And now Daniel testified, "Behold, one like the similitude of the sons of men touched my lips: then I opened my mouth and spoke…Then there came again and touched me one like the appearance of a man, and He strengthened me" (Daniel 10:16, 18). These men's experiences are examples to us all: God is searching for those who will take time to be shut in with him. You may say, "I can't spend hours a day praying. I have obligations like everyone else." Daniel himself was a busy man. As a prominent government official, he had incredible demands on his time. Yet Daniel set his heart to seek the Lord. And he made quality time daily three times a day, in fact to pray. God answered him with an astonishing vision: "I Daniel fainted, and was sick certain days; afterward, I rose up, and did the king's business; and I was astonished at the vision, but none understood it" (Daniel 8:27). Even in sickness, or during his daily business, Daniel sought the Lord.

Recognize the Decline

Daniel grieved over the spiritual decline in society and in the church. There is a hearted attitude in even the most joyous believer that causes him to mourn over the lukewarm condition of the church and the moral decline in our nation. We see this in Daniel's life. At the time, Daniel was receiving visions in the middle of the night. He was miraculously delivered from a lion's den. The Lord was blessing and prospering this man tremendously. Yet all that time, Daniel never put out of mind the grievous things God was showing him about Israel: "I Daniel was grieved in my spirit in the midst of my body, and the visions of my head troubled me" (Daniel 7:15). Over and over Daniel testifies, "These divine words, these visions of the future, troubled me. They stirred my soul and caused me to mourn and grieve." Now God revealed to Daniel that he was about to pluck up every evil thing and cast it down. He would stomp on wicked nations and destroy them. Judgment Day was near, and time was running out — yet, amazingly, God's people were oblivious to it all. So, Daniel began to mourn over the deadness and depravity in God's house.

I see a similar scene in God's house today. Ministers and churches have closed their ears to biblical warnings. They refuse to hear or say anything negative. In their minds, it's time to simply enjoy life. Yet many of these same people once experienced miracles. They prayed for their lost loved ones in the kingdom. They grieved over the moral landslide in society and looked eagerly for Christ's coming. But now they have their own agenda. They will not spend one ounce of energy

51

grieving with God over a dying nation and a lukewarm church. As Scripture says, "They are not grieved for the affliction of Joseph" (Amos 6:6). I tell you, Daniel received God's touch because he was willing to grieve with the Lord. He prayed fervently, "Lord, what is going on? I must understand these times. Show me, so I can warn your people." He did not care if he was mocked. He was consumed with a zeal to know God's heart and share his burden.

Let God Reveal His word.

"I prayed unto the Lord my God, and made my confession, and said, O Lord, the great and dreadful God, keeping the covenant and mercy to them that love him, and to them that keep His commandments; we have sinned, and have committed iniquity, and have done wickedly, and have rebelled, even by departing from thy precepts and from thy judgments" (Daniel 9:4-5). Here is another mark of someone after God's heart: He identifies himself with the church's sins. This servant cries out for holiness, both in himself and in God's people. A church can call for prayer meetings regularly, but without purity, prayer is powerless. The message that God wants to speak to his people must come from lips that have been purged.

I challenge every pastor, every teacher, every lay person: Get desperate for God's touch. Stay in communion with Him and allow the Holy Spirit to examine your heart. He'll expose every wicked, rebellious, sinful thing hidden in you. And He'll deal with you about every area of disobedience. Soon, you'll no longer tolerate hypocrisy or compromise in yourself. Your prayers will turn into cries for holiness. Then, whenever you see sin in God's house, you'll cry, "Oh, Lord, we have sinned against you." That's how you'll know God has touched you. He has begun His divine work of changing you, anointing you afresh, and preparing you for a greater work. I have been called to teach the word of God but not in the way we see every day. While in prayer, while sick unto death in 2021 the doctors in the hospital sent me home to die. I contracted bacteria phenomena during COVID. The Holy Spirit with vision, God went to work showing me the Who, What, When and How. The ability to see Him differently and expound on it differently was another touch. We see a picture of this in Scripture, with Saul's special militia. The Bible tells us, "There went with him a band of men, whose hearts God had touched" (1 Samuel 10:26). Jacob, A Man Touched by God; on his trip to meet Esau, Jacob wrestled with God one night. He would not let go until God blessed him. God intermittently blessed him, but he also touched the socket of his hip, and it came out of joint. This time Jacob was finally convinced God was with him and that He would bless him. He even had proof because from that point on he had a limp on his hip. And He said, "Your name shall no longer be called Jacob, but Israel; for you have struggled with God and with men and have prevailed." Then Jacob asked, saying, "tell me Your name, I pray. "And He said, "Why is it that you ask about My name?" And He blessed him there. So, Jacob called the name of the place Peniel: "For I have seen God face to face, and my life is preserved." Genesis 32:28-30. Some of us like Jacob are hardheaded, and we need a lot of proof. It takes several intermittent encounters with God before we are convinced that He is with us, and that He can handle everything without our help. Jacob was a changed man because this time God's touch was so tangible that he wasn't going to forget it anymore. The Lord also changed Jacob's name. He was not going to be known by his past as a deceiver anymore, but he was going to be identified by his future, the nation of Israel coming out of his descendants! Praise God that when we submit our lives to Jesus, He speaks words of life to us; He declares truth for our future. The Lord calls us by what we are becoming not what we used to be in the past. Years later, Jacob's own sons deceived him about Joseph and his disappearance. Is it possible that Jacob reaped deception and supplanting by his sons because he sowed those seeds in his relationship with his brother years prior? Sometimes, we like to think that when we repent God takes away all our sins and their consequences. The Lord does remove our sins, but He doesn't necessarily take away the consequences of our sins. That's why it's important not to play with sin because the consequences can go on for years or generations. Praise God that he gave Jacob the opportunity to finally discover the truth about Joseph and be reunited with him before he died. God was faithful to Jacob and fulfilled His promises in his life.

Have you been resistant to change in an area of your life despite all His reassurances? What will it take for you to believe in the Lord in that area? What is the price you're willing to pay for doing it your own way? Do you believe God concerning your future? Are you cooperating with the Lord through obedience or are you trying to help Him through your own ingenuity?

Lord, help us to see the error of our ways quickly and turn to you humbly and willingly.

TIME CHANGE

Thanks for the rain that falls.
Thanks for the wind that blows.
For the winter that chills
When these bleak days burst
Into spring beauty.
They teach us a valuable lesson –
That Nothing lasts forever.
Likewise, I have learned to appreciate, that difficult times
Are seasons that yield Laughter and joy.

Chapter 7

Intermittent Knowledge Christ and Marriage

God says, "And the Lord God caused a deep sleep to fall upon Adam, and he slept: and He took one of his ribs and  closed the flesh instead thereof; And the rib, which the Lord God had taken from man, made He a woman, and brought her unto the man." Genesis 2:21,22. Gooden expounds, it was not until the holy spirit showed him the connection of Christ to the Church that his eyes were opened to the revelation of how a man is to love his wife.

Should we dare tell the whole truth?

Often, people fear telling the whole truth when it goes against common convention. Also, there is a lot of demonic push back from the evil one when fundamental truths are set straight. However, if we are ever to mature in Christ, we must have the courage to plainly tell others what the Spirit is saying to this generation. We all have little understanding about Divine Love. We, as it were, see through a glass darkly in intimacy, but Godly intimacy is perhaps the opaquest of all.

In the beginning, God made Eve for Adam, and she was taken out of him and then brought back to him to be his helpmate. God is the one who authored their relationship. It was a divine institution to marriage. We clearly see other divine unions in the Old Testament; Abraham and Sarah, Isaac and Rachael, Boaz and Ruth, and Joseph and Mary just to name a few. God authored and approved all these relationships. Through these unions, God brought forth children who would bless nations. These godly relationships were more than mere physical unions, they were unions that produced offspring according to God's plan. These divine unions for humanity were not random pairings but matches made in heaven. Through foreknowledge, according to the wisdom of our Father, God can help us choose our mate. This is one major choice we make in life as husband and wife that impacts our usefulness to God and influences the community and our growth in Him. Marriage partners, equally yoked according to the Spirit of God, help us reach our full potential in Him.

Does God have complete sovereignty over your life?

I ask you, if we are bought at a price and we are not our own, is the choice of whom we marry up to us? Shouldn't we allow God to lead and guide us in every area of our lives? Marriage is one of the most critical decisions we ever make; therefore, our choice of spouse cannot be entered into without the express guidance of our Father. Does God have complete sovereignty in our union and what does divine union mean in "real" life? First, it means that we must seek the will of the Holy Spirit for our choice of mates. Secondly, it means that we must allow God to connect us with our future wife or husband. We cannot allow outward appearances or worldly attributes to be the determining factor in romance. Beauty fades and fortunes change, but a mate that God chooses endures forever. Literally, we must pray and ask for God's blessing on our choice of spouse. We must trust God's voice more than we trust our emotions and personal desires. God tries the hearts of men and women. Only God knows what we are made of. The Holy Spirit is the only one qualified to give an accurate recommendation of who will be a proper fit in our life. How do we know what "true love is? We are constantly drawn by the enticement of the world around us, this makes it a challenge to discern lust from love. God can draw people together through many different avenues. The circumstances of how you get there aren't important; it's the outcome of true love. True love is a divinely appointed set of circumstance intended to get you where God wants you...intentionally. God then intermittently makes His will be understood through divine love, which powerfully joins two people together. True love is a taste of the first love of Eden, and its power is legendary. Gooden admits. I didn't understand this when I sought out to be married, thus not knowing Christ, and fully understanding myself let alone what marriage was about I suffered divorce. In the end, unless you fully understand the consequences of marriage and what it really entitles it's best to seek counsel before engaging and causing more harm than good. God established a remedy for us to have successful marriages, however many of us have entered marriage against Christ. Marrying unwisely may alter your eternal destiny. We must allow God to help us choose wisely when it comes to deciding whom we will marry. Let God join you together in divine marriage so that no man will ever put it asunder.

Touched

I further believe, we must stop asking of marriage what God never designed it to be...this perfect union of happiness, conflict-free living, and idolatrous obsession, Gooden explains. Instead, he says, we can appreciate what God designed marriage to provide: partnership, spiritual intimacy, and the ability to pursue God together. So, what do I think is the most common misconception Christians have about marriage? "Finding a 'soul mate' someone who will complete us," he says. "The problem with looking to another human to complete us is that, spiritually speaking, it's idolatry. We are to find our fulfillment and purpose in God...If we expect our spouse to be 'God' to us, he or she will fail every day. No person can live up to such expectations. Everyone has bad days, yells at his or her spouse or is downright selfish. Despite these imperfections, God created the husband and wife to steer each other in His direction. Gooden offers an example: "I have now learned, when my wife forgives me . . . and accepts me, I learn to receive God's forgiveness and acceptance as well. In that moment, she is modeling God to me, revealing God's mercy to me, and helping me to see with my own eyes a very real spiritual reality."

Marriage is a focus on your Spouse.

It is easy to see why God designed love to be focused on another instead of self-centered union patterned after the world. Living that way is a challenge when bills pile up, communication breaks down and you're just plain irritated with your husband or wife. For those days, Gooden offers these reminders to help ease the tension:

- God created marriage as a loyal partnership between one man and one woman.
- Marriage is the firmest foundation for building a family.
- God designed sexual expression to help married couples build intimacy.
- Marriage mirrors God's covenant relationship with His people.

We see this last parallel throughout the Bible. For instance, Jesus refers to himself as the "bridegroom" and to the kingdom of heaven as a "wedding banquet."

These points demonstrate that God's purposes for marriage extend far beyond personal happiness. Gooden is quick to clarify that God is not against happiness, but that marriage promotes even higher values.

58

God did not create marriage just to give us a pleasant means of repopulating the world and providing a steady societal institution to raise children. Further, He planted marriage among humans yet another signpost pointing to His own eternal, spiritual existence."

Serving your spouse

Gooden exclaims from time-to-time irritating habits to weighty issues that seem impossible to resolve, will peak its head up, loving one's spouse through the tough times is not easy. But the same struggles that drive us apart intermittently also shed light on what we value in marriage. "If happiness is our primary goal, we'll get a divorce as soon as happiness seems to wane," Gooden says. "If receiving love is our primary goal, we'll dump our spouse as soon as they seem to be less attentive. But if we marry for the glory of God, to model His love and commitment to our children, and to reveal His witness to the world, divorce makes no sense." Couples who've survived a potentially marriage-ending situation, such as infidelity or a life-threatening disease, may continue to battle with years of built-up resentment, anger, or bitterness. So, what are some ways to strengthen a floundering relationship or even encourage a healthy one? Gooden offers these intermittent practical tips:

- Focus on your spouse's strengths rather than their weaknesses.
- Encourage rather than criticize.
- Pray for your spouse instead of gossiping about them.
- Learn and live what Christ teaches about relating to and loving others.

Young couples, and seasoned ones can benefit from this advice. After all, many of us are not adequately prepared to make the transition from seeing one another several times a week to suddenly sharing everything. Odds are annoying habits and less-than-appealing behaviors will surface. Yet as Christians, we are called to respect one another.

Marriages Intermittently need God's grace and Mercy.

Gooden adds, "The image He uses is Christ Marriage to the Church and how to learn what it means to Die for it. That is, when we are frustrated or angry, instead of pulling back, we must still pursue our partner under God's mercy and grace. Gooden suggests praying this helpful prayer: Lord, how can I love my spouse today like she has never been loved unless I have learned to love you first?

I can't tell you how many times God has given me very practical advice from taking over the cleaning of the house to doing a few loads of laundry," Gooden says. "It's one prayer that I find gets answered just about every time. "While other marriage books may leave us feeling overwhelmed, providing pages of "relationship homework," The Scriptures makes it clear that any couple can have a successful, happy and a holy marriage when a man is touched by God. The Christ-centered relationship, centered around attitude, and an unwavering commitment to making it work, your marriage can flourish just as God designed.

Chapter 8

The Intermittent touch of Wisdom

Solomon understood that "fear of the Lord is the beginning of all wisdom" (Proverbs 9:10). Even though he was lauded for his wisdom, he also realized that with much wisdom comes much grief.

If Any man lack Wisdom let him ask of God

 God gave King Solomon "wisdom and very great insight, and a breadth of understanding as measureless as the sand on the seashore" (1 Kings 4:29). Solomon followed the reign of his beloved father, David, with a reign of wisdom so famous that news spread to distant shores. The Queen of Sheba, "ruler of the kingdom of Saba (or Sheba) in southwestern Arabia," sought out the man behind the rumor. "The Wisdom of Solomon" is another name for the Book of Proverbs in which readers find advice and direction about how to live wisely before God.

The Proverbs are known, even by many unbelievers. This book of the Bible goes by both names because of the sage advice found there. In secular culture and literature, "A proverb is a brief, simple, and popular saying, or a phrase that gives advice and effectively embodies a commonplace truth based on practical experience or common sense." In common usage, one might refer to vernacular wisdom or the sayings of Confucius as "proverbs." Some of Solomon's many wise and simple messages of truth slipped into wider culture such as, "Pride comes before a fall" (Proverbs 16:8) and "A soft answer turns away wrath" (Proverbs 15:1). In other words, The

Proverbs are "An intermittent snapshot guide to life. "Submit your whole mind to the Scripture. Don't think you know better than God's word. Bring it to bear in every area of life. Become a person under authority." The Proverbs describe how to worship and obey God. They show what someone who loves God looks like. Proverb means. A short pithy saying in frequent and widespread use that expresses a basic truth or practical precept.

Gooden underscores the wisdom that God imparted during a close encounter with death in December 2021; gave him another insightful and perspective look into his life, which fractured his thinking towards the importance of not living on past experiences but allowing the past and present to open his spirit to a deeper understanding of the word of Christ through the holy spirit. The new insightfulness had a piercing effect through the dark corners of his life that weren't as visible but would manifest in several ways. He had to take responsibility and view life differently and seriously. He had to fully understand seasons, which required another intermittent touch of wisdom and understanding. Wisdom to be what he was to represent in the world around him, so he believed in seeking the Lord's wisdom; from his mouth came a different perspective of knowledge and understanding. He also took note; and reviewed and renewed his choices and made changes as required. We all must listen for God's voice in everything we do, everywhere we go; He's the one who will keep us on track; Gooden says his life' decisions were out of desperation and aspiring to be something he was not until God touched him. I further had to learn how to handle pressure intelligently much like this story. Consider two women, one whose baby had died, the other claiming the grieving mother had stolen her baby. The King's plan pretending he would have the baby cut in two drew out the truth. "When all Israel heard the verdict, the king had given, they held the king in awe, because they saw that he had wisdom from God to administer justice" (1

Kings 3:28). "It is not good to be partial to the wicked and so deprive the innocent of justice" (Proverbs 18:5). Life will put you in circumstances that will test your allegiance to the truth of God.

The Wisdom of Solomon and Christ

Solomon worshiped God, for a time. "He said, 'The Lord God of Israel is worthy of praise because He has fulfilled what He promised my father David'" (1 Kings 8:15). Proverbs attest to the fact that, originally, Solomon understood that "fear of the Lord is the beginning of all wisdom" (Proverbs 9:10). Even though he was lauded for his wisdom, observers recognized that his wisdom was too much to be an earthly inheritance; "he had wisdom from God." The Wisdom of Solomon or "Proverbs" is an Old Testament equivalent of Christ's parables. Solomon is not a Christ-like figure, even though "proverb" can also be defined as "parable." We see some parallels: Solomon was obedient to God, building the temple as instructed. Christ, of course, was "obedient even to the death of the cross" (Philippians 2:8). We see in Proverbs a promising understanding of God's character and God's expectations of everyone, the King included. Yet, Solomon's wisdom eventually gave way to the piercing effect of temptation: for power, fame, and wealth. "It was gradual. No man becomes abandoned or altogether depraved at once; formation of character is, both in its construction and destruction, a gradual process." Christ was sinless from the beginning of His life until the end.

Chapter 9

Piercing the light with Darkness ...the Fall

In the garden of Eden, Satan recognized the power and unity that Adam and Eve inherited within their relationship,  and because of his jealousy, he devised a plan to use a quality placed within each of them to pit them against each other and God, thus convincing Eve to fulfill herself (vs. 6). Adam followed and fulfilled his flesh. He listened to her without regard to what the Lord God had said (vs.17). Selfishness is mentioned for the first time in scripture after the fall. No longer had the nature of God ruled, they each began to fulfill selfishness at the expense of the other. Covered themselves from each other (Genesis 3:7); and they were no longer transparent before each other. This pattern continues today as couples protect themselves and hide from each other. Hidden from God (Genesis 3:8), they no longer feared God and no longer saw Him as part of their marriage. I must admit during the divorce from my kids' mother, I failed to recognize the enemy and lost sight of the fact, that God must be the center and foundation of my life. Like Adam, I became confused as to whom my enemy was (Genesis 3:12), therefore I failed to recognize Satan as my enemy, but blamed others. Many couples today are also tricked by the enemy into thinking that the problem is their spouse. The darkness will cause you to justify your sin and perpetuate the problem (Genesis 3:12). We must never fail to admit our fault in the sin; and never justify it, and repent. Eden intermittently deteriorated over time and only the physical union was left (Genesis 4:1). Polygamy, multiple concubines, division, and divorce increased throughout the Old Testament. Finally, Moses required a written divorce decree to keep matters straight (Deuteronomy 24:1). The call to intermittently redeem mankind came through Jesus Christ as the remedy to restore mankind back to original relationship with God that Adam had lost (Romans 5:18; 2 Corinthians 5:15). He also redeemed marriage lost at the fall. (Galatians 3:13, Christ redeemed us from the curse of the law. He renewed the original standards for marriage (Matthew 19:3-9; Mark 10:2-12; Luke 16:15,18). The Pharisees tried to trap Jesus regarding the Mosaic Law (Matthew 19:7). Jesus did not clarify Mosaic Law. He used God's original plan for His point of reference. Divorce was permitted when hearts were hardened. I now had to understand the pre-redemption conditions. Jesus came to change hardened hearts (Jeremiah 32:39; Ezekiel 11:19). The original plan of God did not include separation or divorce; "but from the beginning it was not so" (Matthew 19:8 KJV). Jesus gave no excuse for divorce when He was talking privately to His disciples in Mark 10:1 1,12 and said that remarriage is adultery.

I had to accept there is therefore no Condemnation (Romans 8:1) If you have experienced divorce and remarriage as a Christian, forgive yourself; I had to forgive myself to be free.

Thought to Ponder

Once sin is confessed and you have received forgiveness, do not allow the enemy to harass you anymore regarding this issue. From this time forth, your testimony will line up with the word of God. It will not be a stumbling block to others but will be a clear trumpet sound regarding God's heart for marriages. Forgiveness is about letting go of anger and your desire for revenge. Realize that you are powerless to forgive unless you have God's strength. God does not ask you to do something without giving you His strength and power to do it (Psalm 29:11). Proceed from this point today and let the past go.

Gooden further elaborates on this revelation in the understanding of the darkness piercing the light and how Christ  took the fall of man and wrapped all things into His plan of redemption. It's that moment in time that we got to gleam into the purpose, and priority of polarity. To explain this, we all must understand that God in His own purpose has set the stage of all things. The standard operational procedures are set forth and have been from the beginning. Gooden refers to it as the Polarity of Differences, simply understood as; two opposing viewpoints, neither of which is "right" or "wrong," but which may cause tension or strong feelings between proponents of one viewpoint and the other. Those involved understand that both perspectives have some merit – an "either/or" solution will not work. For any successful relationship packed with sexual attraction and deep connection, there's polarity. Gooden says think about the most passionate relationships of the people you know well. How masculine or feminine are they? If you think about it well enough, you'll realize that they operate under the law of polarity. Simply put, it's the male and female not male or female. It's never up or down but up and down of circumstances. I had to be renewed in the spirit of my mind. The understanding of things I could not grasp in my limited understanding, had to be formatted through and in of the spirit of Christ. Thus, embracing that God created all things and that all things are created and intended for His purpose. Only in Jesus can we receive all God has for marriage. He is the only one who has purchased back that which was lost through Adam and Eve and without Jesus, marriage can only be a counterfeit of what God intends. We are born with selfish, earthy tamed natures. Therefore, we must be born again (John 3:3) and recognize that without Jesus, we can only strive to improve ourselves with worldly techniques and methods, which I identify as polarity of different masks, that we put on to attain certain goals we think we can't reach being our authentic selves. The masks will lead to problems from incompatible relationships to depolarized ones. For instance, a feminine girl might be

66

taught to become masculine by her parents who think feminine ladies won't make it in this harsh world. She starts developing a masculine mask which she uses to protect herself in the future with her masculine partners and ruins her romantic relationships. Consequently, a boy with a masculine core might also be taught that masculine traits are toxic, especially by a feminine caregiver who confused healthy masculine traits with toxic ones like manipulation and aggression. He might develop a feminine mask and start caring about his looks too much, become too emotional and the like which repulses feminine partners in the future. At the end of the day, a masculine man would best fit into a masculine role and a feminine woman would best bring a feminine essence to a romantic relationship. Only Jesus can change hearts. Marriage redeemed in Jesus need not conform to earthly standards nor be plagued by those things that are destroying marriages around us. When we are one in Christ our vision for marriage our homes become the oasis of peace and power that God intended. We must remember, God created Adam in His image. Adam was whole and complete. Genesis 2:22. Eve was taken from Adam, not formed separately. Each one retained the quality that the other needed. Man and woman are created to be complementary, not competing. After the fall, it was no longer possible to discern God's plan by observing earthly couples. God gave example for marriage based in the relationship of Christ, the bride groom and the Church, His Bride in Ephesians 5:22-33. The roles of husband and wife can be understood by observing Jesus and the Church's interaction. Jesus/husband and Church/wife roles. This is not intended to compare redemptive roles in Jesus. We are many members but one body in Christ as husband and wife. This is only designed to help you understand your role. Concentrate on God's plan for you. Your responsibility is connected and laced within each one's own ability and owning those abilities given, and not responding outside of our primary assignment and or purpose. The garden of Eden is established under the process of intermittently leaving and cleaving (Genesis 2:24) which is based on covenant, and does not mean severing relationships, but understanding why Jesus left His Father to establish a covenant with the Church to maintain relationship, as with Jesus and the Church, and its primary responsibility. The husband and wife must operate in conjunction with the covenant of being loved, cared for, nurtured, and the giving up of each one's life. Two opposing energies, having the ability to give up all to establish relationship with each other (Philippians 2:6,7).

When God created Adam, He made him complete and whole in His image (Genesis 1.26) By taking Eve from part of Adam, not just forming her separately (Genesis 2. 22), He enabled each one to retain qualities that the other needed. God created man and woman to be complementary to each other and intended that male and female qualities would complement not compete.

After the fall of man, the image of marriage as God intended became clouded. It was no longer possible to discern God's plan by observing the actions of couples. God, therefore, through scripture gave man and woman a heavenly example to follow; Ephesian 5:22-23 gives direction to husband and wife for their unity using the example of Christ, the Bridegroom, and the Church, His bride. The Roles of husband and wife as God intended for them can, therefore, be understood by observing the interaction of Jesus and the Church. These lessons if studied will yield a variety of roles which the husband and wife can utilize in understanding Jesus and the Church as our example. It is not intended, however, in any way to compare the redemptive role of Jesus with that of the husband. It should also be noted that just as Jesus expected the Church to do the same works, He did, so are the roles of husband and wife. Remember also that God has placed within each one of us certain abilities. When we respond to those responsibilities, we can operate in the abilities God has given us. If we attempt to respond in areas that are not our assignments, we are operating out of purpose. Therefore, abide in the calling wherewith Christ has called you. All things considered, when purpose is not known, in darkness, as we understand it, has often been misunderstood with adversities, tribulation, and falling. I would like to submit to us that until we understand the polarity of differences, we will never be able to reach our intended purpose. The reason for my explanation in this matter is because we are often confused... not realizing that the prefix, Latin word-forming element means "together, with," sometimes merely intensive. Fuse or Fusion has several meanings depending on the context. In general, it means the process or result of joining two or more things together to form a single entity. The interesting definition of the Latin word gives us a better understanding of fuse. This Latin root is the word origin of a good number of English vocabulary words, including fusion, fuse, and confuse. The root fusis easily recalled via the word refuse, for to refuse to do something asked of you is to "pour" the request right back to the person doing the requesting! Listen to what the scripture asked of us and how we are to pour it back. Profiting from Confusion/Trials, my brethren, count it all joy when you fall into various trials, knowing that the testing of your faith produces patience. But let patience have its perfect work, that you may be perfect and complete, lacking nothing. If any of you lacks wisdom, let him ask of God, who gives to all liberally and without reproach, and it will be given to him. But let him ask in faith, with no doubting, for he who doubts is like a wave of the sea driven and tossed by the wind. For let not that man suppose that he will receive anything from the Lord; he is a double-minded man, unstable in all his ways. Once I understood the polarity of differences, it fractured my thinking into a realm of wisdom through Christ and the awareness of His plan for all things. Therefore, I had to embrace what we call darkness i.e., trials and tribulation and or anything negative that happens. The question now becomes is it really a problem or a polarity? We all must address this individually. Every day we waste energy and create pain from misdiagnosing a paradox and treating it as a problem to solve and then fighting over the two poles." Polarities are ongoing, chronic issues that are unavoidable and unsolvable. Attempting to address them with traditional problem-solving skills only makes things worse." Polarities always contain problems to solve. Problems to solve can be a part of a polarity, and they can have polarities within them. "Example: What happens if you focus too much on activity at the expense of rest? You get the downside of injury, if you over-focus on one pole or the other, to neglect of its partner, first you get the downside of the pole on which you over-focus, then you get the downside of the other pole as well. What keeps us from moving from one pole to another is our fear of the downside of the pole we're moving towards. And the fear is that we're going to lose the upside of the pole we're moving from, confused. The depolarizing effect of sin has intermittently blinded us to our intended purpose in Christ, diminishing our relationship polarity due to the absence of not accepting opposing energy. This happens when we ditch our spiritual/positive energy and take on the natural/negative energy of external forces.

Once I began to allow the differences of Polarities, I understood the polarizing effect of polarities. Jesus as the catalyst of crisis, a polarizing, divisive, and destabilizing force. His coming forces people to choose a side, to reveal their deepest allegiances, to show hands previously held close to chests. His destiny leads to the fall and to the rising again, resurrection of many within the nation. In the process, hearts are revealed. The Husband, and wife, relationships must be priority over all other earthy relationships and the husband must provide her all the Kingdom of God offers:

1) Luke 12:32; 9:10-17, *forgives her.*
2) Luke 23:34, *Heals her.*
3) Luke 4:38-41; Matthew 8: 14~17; Mark 1:29-34), *Serves her.*
4) John 13:1-7; Philippians 2:4), *Leads her.*
5) Luke 9:23; Joshua 24:15), *Gives Godly purpose to lives.*
6) Luke 5:8-10, *Intercedes for her.*
7) Luke 5:16; Luke 6:12; Hebrews 7:25), *Comforts her.*
8) Mark 6:34, *Exhorts and encourages her.*
9) Luke 12:35- 48, *Gives her strength.*
10) Luke 8:22—25, *Be example of God's heart.*
11) John 14:9; John 17:10), *Teaches her.*
12) Luke 4:31,32, 6:27-35; Matthew7,1-28,29; Luke 11:1-4), *Respects authority*
13) Luke 20:20 26, *Opposes sin.*
14) Luke 19:45, 20:45-47), *Discerns spirits.*
15) Luke 5:22 *Has authority over spiritual darkness* (Luke 4:36).

Piercing the darkness of lying. No Secrets

I preference this touch from God as one that most men will not be able to attest to, because we haven't truly committed  our lives to Christ and have more attachment to this world and its carnal ways. The wisdom I proclaim is God's secret wisdom, which is hidden from human beings, but which He had already chosen for our glory even before the world was made. When Christ has taken control of us it's amazing what happens to our will, and His will be done. The intermittent touch of honesty piercing your old nature becomes a choice and an action that leads to experiencing love and loving others with your true self. If we fail to be real and transparent in our marriage, we fail ourselves and ultimately each other. Lies are culprits of painful marriages. The reality of the matter is we do not want our good to be evil spoken of, so, avoid the very appearance of outside circumstances, which will come to test and threaten our marriage. We cannot control outside forces, but we can dress ourselves appropriately, by choosing honesty as the catalyst to open communication in our marriages. How can we be one if we are not honest about everything? How can we strategize our next move if all the cards aren't on the table? To work together, we need to be real with one another. Christ said that He is the Way, the Truth, and the Life. If Christ is Truth, then it follows that lying is moving away from Christ. Being honest is about following in God's footsteps, for He cannot lie. If our goal is to become more God-like and God-centered, then honesty must be the theme of our focus.

Hebrews 6:18 - "So God has given both his promise and his oath. These two things are unchangeable because it is impossible for God to lie."

Honesty Reveals Our Character

Honesty is a direct reflection of your inner character. Your actions reflect your faith, and reflecting the truth in your actions is a part of being a good witness. Learning how to be more honest will also help you keep a clear consciousness. Character plays a big role in where you go in your life. Honesty is considered a characteristic that employers and college interviewers look for in candidates. When you are faithful and honest, it shows.

Luke 16:10 - "Whoever can be trusted with very little can also be trusted with much, and whoever is dishonest with very little will also be dishonest with much."

1 Timothy 1:19 - "Cling to your faith in Christ and keep your conscience clear. For some people have deliberately violated their consciences; as a result, their faith has been shipwrecked." (NLT)

72

Proverbs 12:5 - "The plans of the righteous are just, but the advice of the wicked is deceitful." (NIV)

We need to remove our masks and choose to be honest. This way we can embrace each other, link arms, and face life together as intended from the beginning. I have fully come to understand that marriage must be a place where you take off all your masks. When you said your vows, you committed your whole self to your spouse. You committed your love in all circumstances, for (richer, poorer, sickness, and in health, you do remember). You chose to share your inner self with your spouse. You cannot love a mask, and neither can your spouse. The only way to experience love is when you are vulnerable through Christ. Vulnerability is attained through honesty and transparency in the communication of your relationship. You cannot do this in and of yourself. I must admit, it was hard to trust throughout most of my life, when deception is all, you encounter. I finally realized that a spouse cannot truly know you if you fail to be transparent in the relationship. Arguably, you also may not know yourself. When we choose dishonesty, our spouse is robbed of the opportunity to love. Honesty encourages growth and adds a depth to relationships that cannot be replicated. Transparency builds a strong foundation in marriage, creating trust. Honesty says, "We are one". Transparency implies openness, communication, and accountability. In short transparency is not hiding anything. Whether things are good or bad, you openly and honestly convey information as you know.

Gooden said his transparency gave his wife an opportunity to know him and to respond. It gave her the chance to be vulnerable and secure. She responded in love, no need for pretentiousness when I surrendered to honesty. Now we can be one in Christ, conquering life together. I feel safer knowing I am not alone.

Chapter 10

A Faithful Man Who Can Find?

Gooden elaborates unfaithfulness takes on many characteristics, it's not always sex. The word of God says the  weights and the sins that so easily beset us. As men we are found to be asking the question, who can find a virtuous woman. It's easy to cast the light off oneself to dodge the bullet of self-examination. What about the faithful man? The man touched by God isn't perfect put he is faithful. Therefore, men we must ask ourselves if we truly desire to be defined by the Lord our God as good and faithful servants; we must examine ourselves whether we possess that proud spirit wherein we presumptuously perceive and proclaim our "own goodness," or whether we are truly walking in godly integrity before the Lord our God, faithfully fulfilling the responsibilities that He has given to us. Are we maintaining that spirit of pride wherein we proclaim our "own goodness," rather than pursuing and producing godly faithfulness, let us be zealous to repent thereof. *"Most men will proclaim everyone his own goodness: but a faithful man who can find?"* A proverbial statement cannot be defined as a short, meaningful saying that expresses a significant, substantial truth for life. In the book of Proverbs, a proverb is often constructed with two lines, presenting a comparison or contrast. Proverbs 20:6 presents a truth of contrast. Whereas the great majority of men will boldly proclaim their own goodness, a truly faithful man is a quite rare and precious find. Gooden interprets the first line of this proverb are "most men." The subject in the second line of this proverb is "a faithful man." Thus, the contrast of this proverb concerns the character of most men in opposition to the character of a truly faithful man. However, the contrast of this proverb is not structured in the form of a direct parallel. Rather, the first line of the proverb makes a statement of truth concerning "most men, whereas the second line of the proverb asks a rhetorical question concerning the truly faithful man. So then, what does the opening statement of truth in this proverb reveal concerning most men? This opening statement reveals three basic elements concerning the nature of men that is – concerning the natural character of men.

First, it reveals that men in their natural character are proud of, and preferential to themselves. Yea, this proverb states, "Most men will proclaim everyone his own goodness." Indeed, men in their natural character focus their attention upon what they perceive about how good they are. This is a spirit of pride concerning oneself. In addition, men in their natural character focus their attention upon their own perceived goodness, while ignoring the possible goodness of others. This is a spirit of proud preference for oneself. Consequentially, this is the nature of "most men."

Second, the opening statement of truth in this proverb reveals that men in their natural character promote and praise up themselves. Yea, this proverb states, "Most men will proclaim everyone his own goodness." Indeed, men in their natural character will not only focus the attention of their own proud hearts upon what they perceive about how good they are; but they will also proclaim this viewpoint in daily communication. Men's natural character will proclaim how good they perceive themselves to be. They will promote themselves. They will praise themselves. Yea, this is the nature of "most men."

Third, the contrast between the opening statement of truth in this proverb and the rhetorical question of this proverbs reveals that men in their natural character are presumptuous and pretentious concerning themselves. While stating in the opening line of the proverb that "most men" will proudly and boldly proclaim their own goodness, this proverb indicates through the rhetorical question that a truly "faithful man" is quite rare among the multitude of men – "But a faithful man who can find?" Thus, we are moved to understand that "most men" are not actually in the category of the "faithful man." Although men in their natural character will proclaim their own goodness, they are not actually as good and faithful as they proclaim. Gooden exclaim we are born and shaped in iniquity; indeed, we are not good and faithful at all. Rather, we are presumptuous in that we simply take our own goodness for granted, as an obvious and absolute truth simply because we perceive it to be so. In addition, we are pretentious in our perception and proclamation of our own goodness. So then, we are brought to understand through this proverbial contrast that it is not what a man perceives of his character, which is often filled with the self-deception of pride; or what a man proclaims concerning his character that truly matters; rather, it is what a man produces in his daily conduct that truly matters; for faithfulness in his God-given responsibilities is that which defines a truly "good" man. Yet truly good and faithful men are hard to find, because so few of us men truly pursue faithfulness in our daily walk. This then is truly the need for men to embrace godly faithfulness with the responsibilities as disciples to walk in righteousness, because we have been truly touched by God.

Gooden further communicates that he had to learn how to live faithfully daily, therefore dying to the lust of the eyes and the pride of life. The integration of the proverbial context that surrounds God and man is established in Proverbs 20:6 which appears to present truths and warnings with a focus upon the negative perspective. This more negative perspective appears to begin at Proverbs 19:24 and to extend unto Proverbs 20:25.

As such, we find various characteristics that would be contrary to the character and conduct of the faithful men," but would be true for the character of most men. The "faithful man" is not a lazy, slothful man, does not dishonor his parents, rejects ungodly counsel but heeds godly counsel, is not an ungodly witness, is not a spiritual fool or scorner, is not deceived by alcohol, does not rebel against government authority, does not meddle in strife, is not deceitful in business. does not have vengeful spirit. Rather, the "faithful man" will pursue and maintain godly integrity in his character, in his conduct and in his communication (Proverbs 20:15).

WHAT WILL YOU CHOOSE

You're hanging in the balance of heaven and hell.
captured now by Satan's spell. Many doors that you might
choose Take the wrong one, and your soul,
you'll lose. It's not a game that Satan plays,
as he draws your mind into a maze. It's true that the wages of
sin is death and hell a reality not just a myth.
Choose this day whom you will serve.
Let Jesus Christ your soul preserve.
How could you trade his priceless treasure for just a few
moments of fleeting pleasure?
Life here is short, oh why can't you see.
It's nothing compared to eternity.
Look up, reach out and take Gods hand.
And he'll lead you safely to the promised land.
A snare for your soul, did the enemy weave.
But you can be set free,
Only trust and believe.

Chapter 11

The Purpose of a Beautiful Touch

As Gooden reflect, he states, he would have never understood himself, God, or marriage until he understood the  relationship that Christ had with the Church. He exclaims he might be a self-renowned expert on this subject; he certainly has the knots on his head to prove it. He sought love high and low, always with the greatest hopes; and pursued it with great expectations; however, the results unexpectedly turned into utter despondence. Yet his grief never quite quelled his hope-filled pursuits—for love, as unto priceless rubies.

Looking for Love of Self

But let me reveal something about my quest. Though I have come open hearted in giving love, my love was not always clean. What is human love anyway? But where my love was sullied was in the fact that I responded to reaction. I focused on whether my love was reciprocated or rejected; an often occurrence which I just couldn't understand as a man of God. I am not to respond based on others but in my faith. Piercing the darkness of negative feelings in love; while intermittently being touched by God's love is wide open and not gauged by the response of others. Well, you might say, how in the world am I to respond like that? I will tell you very clearly. When I love for love of Him, and not for love of a person, then I will be set free to <u>love</u>. So, you might ask, "Gooden, are you saying my love for my wife is not about my love for my wife but love for my God?" Yes, that is exactly what I would have said…. It was the catalyst for setting me free to love myself after not knowing love, let alone loving someone. It is for freedom that Christ has set us free.

To stand firm, and not let myself be burdened again by a yoke of pain and suffering inflicted upon me as a child and young adult. … You, my brothers, and sisters, were called to be free. But do not use your freedom to indulge the flesh; rather, serve one another humbly in love. When I understood love, without expectations it freed me from presuppositional loving; because my love was focused on God and pour out of me with purity. The responses of another will not influence my decisions because my love is for Him and indirectly for the other person. I know this is mind-bending, but I believe I can love without being enmeshed. All the love we see on the screen, or in books, or wherever, is mostly codependent and based on self-love. It's looking for love in all the wrong places. What I am talking about is a higher love (Agape). Loving without expectations means being okay enough with yourself to love someone else. It means not feeling insecure when they don't express their love the way you express yours. It means being okay enough with yourself, so you don't have to seek someone else's approval, so that your happiness does not hinge on whether someone else thinks the world of you.

DEAR LORD

In the midst of confusion, endless theories
and varied philosophies; help me find your
laws and statues of life to guide me. Stir within me the
hunger for your word. Amid the storms that
I may change the things I can and accept the
things I cannot. may your spirit grant me the wisdom to know
the difference as I pass through this.
barren land.

Chapter 12

The Power of His Love

The power of His love was intermittently understood and came from all the pain and suffering of my life and is a  continual progression in His intended purpose. We will not fully understand this life, but we can embrace what we have learned through trials and tribulation. If I give another the power to influence something so holy as love in me, then I am giving away the power of love. Love is so much more than just what response someone offers. Love is patient, Love is kind, Love doesn't envy, Love doesn't boast, Love isn't proud, Love isn't rude, Love isn't self-seeking, Love isn't easily angered, Love keeps no record of wrong, Love doesn't delight in evil but rejoices in Truth, Love always protects, always trusts, always hopes, always perseveres—Love never fails because Love is symbolic to Jesus Christ! So, I choose not to squelch the most powerful force of the universe, either through my flawed ego or because of another's receptivity. The Lord Jesus loved fully and totally and showed that towards all creation.

The strongest example of husband and wife is when they share a deep sense of meaning in their flaws but allowing the power of Love to mold them. They don't just "get along" they also support each other's hopes and aspirations and build a sense of purpose into their lives together. That is important. What does it mean when we talk about honoring and respecting each other? Very often a marriage failure of husband and wife is due to unfruitfulness of the spirit and the indulgence of endless, useless rounds of argument which leads to feeling isolated and lonely in their marriage. Relationship quarrels are not about whether the toilet lid is up or down or whose turn it is to take out the trash. They are deeper, hidden issues that fuel these superficial conflicts and make them far more intense and hurtful than they would otherwise be.

Once you understand this, you will be ready to accept one of the most surprising truths about marriage: <u>most marital arguments cannot be resolved</u>. Couples spend year after year trying to change each other's mind, but it can't be done. This is because most of their disagreements are rooted in fundamental differences of lifestyle, personality, or values. By fighting over these differences, all they succeed in doing is wasting their time, therefore harming their marriage, instead, they need to understand the bottom-line difference that is causing the conflict and to learn how to live with it by honoring and respecting each other. Only then will they be able to build shared meaning and a sense of purpose in their marriage. It used to be that couples could achieve this goal only through their own insight, instinct, or blessed luck. But now the Holy Scriptures provides principles that are designed for marital <u>success to all couples</u>. No matter what the current state of your relationship, following the scripture can lead to dramatic, positive change.

The first step toward improving or enhancing your marriage is to understand what happens when the Scriptures are not followed. This has been well documented by Christ Jesus death into couples who were not able to save their marriages or themselves. Learning about the principles of the cross can prevent your marriage from making the same mistakes repeatedly. Once you come to understand that you are more than a conqueror you will know why some marriages fail, and how the principles applied here could prevent such tragedies, you'll be on the way to improving your own marriage forever. So... Now I am giving you a new commandment: Love each other. Just as I have loved you, you should love each other. Your love for one another will prove to the world that you are my disciples (John 13:34-35)." "Submit to one another out of reverence for Christ (Eph. 5:21)." The submitting to one another" in Ephesians 5:21 is addressing the marriage unit. We know this because verse 22 does not have the word "submit" in our earliest manuscripts (written in ancient Greek). Therefore, verse 21 supplies the verb for verse 22. The verses must go together. Regardless, it is evident throughout the New Testament that all believers are called to submit to one another (to give in to one another's wills). To fully understand love, I am proposing we need to know that a successful marriage has little to do with love in and of itself, it has to do with the knowledge of what is and how it is defined. You can feel you love someone or thing, however it's best to know the why and how. To love all that one has to offer, all that you have been and all that you are yet to become, knowing that what we think we create, what we create we become, what we become we express, what we experience we are, what we believed caused our circle of our life to be complete. All marriages should partake of the same nature, power, attributes, and characteristics of Christ relationship with the body of Christ. If you are a child of God, it should be just as natural for you to operate in the gifts of the spirit, as it is for fish to swim, and a bird to fly. 2 Peter 1:4. It is an impossibility for the sustaining element that keeps a tree alive…dirt; or the sustaining element for fish …water, and the sustaining element of man; God to be fulfilled in marriage let alone life.

Our homes should offer a setting in which we may encourage each as husband and wife to step out in a non-threatening place if we make a mistake, we are there to exhort and help each other. Now since God brought us together in marriage it must be our desire to share with other couples the healer and the restorer of all things pure. The Bible contains the prescription for our healing of our marriages and relationships and ultimately of ourselves. It's the source for Gods vision and blueprint for all marriages which enables  couples within reach with the exciting news concerning the ministry of being one in Christ. When we are joined as husband and wife, we are anointed to fulfill the purpose of Christ and the church, with all the responsibilities enabled by the Holy Spirit. This office is intended by God to be a vibrant dynamic state of ever deepening love and growth with God's direction we can truly go from glory to glory in our life together, capturing Gods heart in a world that has totally lost the vision of marriage. This understanding of His divine nature and understanding; intermittently pierced and broke through every corner of my mind around the thought and feeling with regards to, "I am a person worthy of love, "I desire love, and I accept the fact that I do." "I am not weak because I love; I am strong because I know I want love, and I know that I am a person who can be loved and can give love in return." You must tell yourself, "I want love, then trust, that you will find it with time. I know this because, on this special day in 2017, I found that special someone who loved me for who I am, in return I was able to love. I totally submit to lay aside all the weights and my sins. This process was intermittent, to gain a full understanding, let alone embraced what I resented prior, because I did not understand love; therefore, I did not give myself a chance to love or be loved. The ability to love unconditionally meant I could love people in tough times. That meant having the ability to love someone when they're being rude or inconsiderate. It also meant loving my enemies. This love takes work.

Matthew,5:43-48
You have heard people say, "Love your neighbors and hate your enemies." But I tell you to love your enemies and pray for anyone who mistreats you. Then you will be acting like

your Father in heaven. He makes the sun rise on both good and bad people. And He sends rain for the ones who do right and for the ones who do wrong. If you love only those people who love you, will God reward you for that? Even tax collectors love their friends. If you greet only your friends, what's so great about that? Don't even unbelievers do that? But you must always act like your Father in heaven. Luke,6:27 But to you who are willing to listen, I say, love your enemies! Do good to those who hate you. Romans,12:9-10. Be sincere in your love for others. Hate everything that is evil and hold tight to everything that is good. Love each other as brothers and sisters and honor others more than you do yourself.

WHAT IS LIFE?

Is it the air we breathe? What do you feel?
Do you feel the sunrays on a sunny day?
Do you feel the raindrops in the month of May?
Do you smell the flowers in the spring air?
I ask again – what is life. Are you aware?
Do you love or run from everyone?
Do you laugh and play or do you just
live for today? Remember, it will get better!
Why waste time on endless thoughts and pleasures.
What is life? Are you lonely? Are you free?
Do you take time for others?
oh, why can't you see. Are you weak or strong? I ask myself,
where in life do I belong. What is your life?

Chapter 13

Touched by God Through Nehemiah 2:18

This story really resonated with me as God began defragmenting my thoughts and ways. The tearing down of the  structures erected through the mishandling of my parents and people in my life. It was my journey, and although I may not have agreed to it, I had to accept it. The story of a man called to rebuild the city walls of Jerusalem; walls that have been torn down and burned by their enemies. The task was awesome and almost an impossible one. There were many who opposed the word, many who rallied near, and those who were there to rebuild it. The people were placed along the wall, and each rebuilding their own section so that the city might once again be safe and protected. The families faced the constant threat of enemy attack. In fact, when the wall was halfway up, they began holding a weapon in one hand, and working with the other. Not only were they totally devoted to the work they were doing; but they were also actually committed to fighting off the enemy, should it become necessary. Today, the wall of protection in a strong family, and our cities, has been destroyed by the enemies' attack. The disintegration of marriages and families throughout the world and past generations have left us vulnerable. Each family must fight their own battles, without the corporate protection afforded by a strong community. It is once again time to come to rebuild the wall just as in the day of Nehemiah. God is supporting multi-families to rally and restore the safety and security of the home; this is His primary concern. During the time when they were building the wall, the families were to be side-by-side, showing each appointed post, doing their portion of the work.

Today, it is also true that strong marriages and families bring strength to a city. Strong families provide a covering of protection for our churches, communities, and homes; that are broken and in ruin, thus leaving these cities, and churches within them, open and vulnerable to the enemy's attack. When we use Gods plan, His word, His tools, and His scripture principles as our blueprint; it will build a strong healthy hedge of protection around our marriages, and our homes. It is the word of God that provides the blueprint for building a strong family, and marriages. A wall, that the gates of hell, shall not prevail against. The word of God also provides boundaries and standards. This is not a time for us to do what is right, in our own lives. It is time to work together as One in Christ. We cannot do our own thing, through either ignorance or self-will, in doing so we consequently lose Gods protection. No matter where you are at this moment, you may feel as if one of the burnt stones in your marriage could not be used to build a strong wall. (Nehemiah 4:2) You can't listen to the voice of the enemy. Jesus Christ has great plans for you, and desires to rebuild you, in strength and in mind as you submit to the blueprint of God's word. Accept both, his boundaries and his protection and your marriage and your home can be transformed by his power. Perhaps you only have cracks in the walls, small areas of erosion that are beginning to wear way. Do you recognize the need to strengthen your walls and fortify it by allowing God to be your guide? There is no better time to begin building than when problems are first recognized. Minor adjustments here and there will firmly establish your marriage on the rock and solidify the protection of your wall; even if you have a strong marriage, established, and grounded in the word you have much to offer. The strength and stability of your portion of the wall is vital to others. Many times, it is hard to help others build or rebuild any success; if you are not sure exactly how your portion of the wall became so strong. You need to know the blueprint you have followed, so that you might share it with others. Whatever the situation of your marriage, and your home is today, you can be blessed, and grow in the Lord through understanding, and application of His will for your marriage. Nehemiah encouraged the people "do not be afraid of them, remember the Lord, great and awesome, and fight for your brother, your sons, your daughters, your wives, and your homes Nehemiah 4:14. We must sacrifice ourselves along with all other commitment; to obtain certain promises and terms contractually, like we proclaimed on that special day regarding the terms of our marriage covenant, i.e. for better or for worse for richer or poor etc. etc. etc. We must fully understand that our exchange, fused all things into one covenant, all we previously held separately according to 1Corinthians 7:4, declares our bodies are given to each other along with our wealth. The word of God says that the two worlds are gone, and everything belongs to that one union.

As covenant couple, if we do not understand this complete exchange and mutual sharing of everything; certain problems will arise in our marriage causing disappointments centered around money; belonging exclusively to that one person, and not to the covenant relationship. In doing so, strife and division can manifest itself and build a wedge in the relationship, losing the primary concern of both partners. We must understand that the marriage covenant automatically signals death to independent living when we enter Gods plan for marriage. It took on a new meaning therefore our singleness of thinking must take on a new direction for the covenant to survive. Covenant demands that the need of your spouse had to be placed before your own and each spouse then had the right to hold the other to the term and promises of our covenant marriage which is also sealed with an oath or vow, such as" I do" or "I will." Marriage vows should be taken serious as the word of God proclaims, "it is better not to vow at all then to vow and not keep our word" (Ecclesiastics 5:4,5).

Intermittently Touched.

The touch of being established through Christ; meant  cooperative action of a discrete agent of accepting the total effects is greater than the sum of the two effects taken independently. The whole is greater than the sum of the parts and that each had unique qualities and attributes that enhanced their unit. The unity of Adam and Eve's combined power and ability was greater (Deuteronomy 32:30). Alone, Adam cultivated and kept the garden (Genesis 2:15), Adam and Eve together filled the earth. subdued it and ruled over...every living thing (Genesis 1:28 NIV). The union of one-flesh is a benefit of the covenant (Genesis 2:24). We are a 3-part being (1 Thessalonians 5:23). Adam and Eve had total unity of the three-part being Spirit, Soul, and body. The body (flesh). Physical one-flesh unity is easiest for us to understand. "And they shall be one flesh" (Genesis 2:24 KJV)." Be fruitful and multiply" (Genesis 1:28 KJV). The Soul intellect, emotions, will. Hardest to achieve. Adam and Eve...were not ashamed, (Genesis 2:25). (The Hebrew definition for "a shame " is translated in other parts of Old Testament as "confused.") For there to have been no confusion between them, they must have had total agreement in the soul realm. We through the spirit joined to the body of Christ, are automatically joined in spirit, knowing Adam and Eve, were created in the image of God and therefore had the unity of His Spirit. The Lord made them one? Therefore, our walk must be nurtured and nourished to mature, to honor, and esteem the needs of our covenant partner over our own. Ephesians 5:28 NIV...he who loves his own wife loves his own soul, as we minister to each other, we nurture our one-flesh relationship. We must acknowledge the foundation of the Kingdom's explosive growth during this intermittent period, the kingdom will also experience explosive growth as we understand each other through the gospel and live out our faith amongst each other and unbelievers. The parable of the mustard seed in Matthew 13:31-32 illustrates this. In it, Christ described the kingdom as a mustard seed which, though tiny, grew into a tree. When this happened, the birds of the air perched in its branches. The seed growing into a tree represents the explosive growth of marriages, family, in respect to the church. After Christ's death, there were 120 followers praying together in one room when the Holy Spirit came at Pentecost in Acts 2. Almost immediately after, 3,000 were saved (Acts 2:41), which soon grew to 5,000 (Acts 4:4). When persecution came, the gospel spread throughout Jerusalem, Judea, Samaria, and to the ends of the earth. Though persecuted, they grew and continue to grow. Currently, Christianity is the biggest religion in the world: 31.2% of the world's population, which equals about 2.3 billion people. Where are we today? Let us not think more of ourselves than we are. The polarity of events in Genesis 2:25 contains revelation concerning God's plan and potential of our lives, especially as husband and wife. They were together as, man and wife. (Genesis 2:24 is the covenant verse-forsaking all others.)"Both" indicates equality before God (also Gal.3:28). No shame or darkness (sin) between them. Imagine being naked, in all ways, physically, emotionally, and spiritually with your spouse with no shame or confusion! That is God's plan for one-flesh living. "Transparent" in spirit, soul, and body; free to be themselves, openly and honest. However, with that said, many believe the birds perched on the branches represent evil within the church. In a previous parable—The parable of the Sowers of the seed (Matt 13:1-23), the birds, as explained by Christ, represented the devil. Therefore, though the kingdom would experience this rapid growth from humble beginnings, it will be polluted with evil, as seen in church corruption, false teachers, and cults, among other manifestations of evil. Though the final stage of the kingdom will be perfect, the current stage is not. This corruption will cause many to fall away from the faith and keep many from ever accepting the faith and accepting each other. The final stage of this kingdom will begin at Christ's return as He establishes His eternal rule on the earth. He will judge sin and restore peace and righteousness in creation. The righteous will rule with Christ for eternity. Revelation 11:15 says: "Then the seventh angel blew his trumpet, and there were loud voices in heaven saying: 'The kingdom of the world has become the kingdom of our Lord and of his Christ, and he will reign for ever and ever. 'Established at creation, lost at the fall, prophesied throughout the Old Testament, currently present in spiritual form, one day, the kingdom will be a physical reality on earth. Lord, let your kingdom come, your will be done on earth as it is in heaven (Matt 6:10)! One of the things that makes the bible unique is its themes: the theme of God's revelation, sin and its consequences, God rewarding faith and obedience, election, Jesus Christ, covenant, and kingdom.

THE TAPPING OF THE RAIN

It was but an hour into the day,
before the rain came dripping my way.
A drop here and a drop there,
Oh, what sudden despair.
Gazing out of this window in total dismay,
I stare.
alone without a care.
When will it stop and where shall I go?
Can you stop the rain from falling?
Can you stop these tears of fear?
Upon the window of my soul?
The sudden touch peace, with a warm embrace left without
A trace.
The tapping of the rain.
Upon the window of my soul.

Chapter 14

Intermittent Role as Husband

The burden of final leadership responsibility for the outcome of his family lies with the husband. A man who  exercises, in love, the authority given him by God will bring strength and stability to his wife and family. Led of the Spirit and directed by the Father, you are to be an example of standing firm despite circumstances. You are to resist the enemy, not your family, and to treat what the Lord speaks to your wife with the same respect that you treat what you personally receive from Him (Luke 8:22- 25, Luke 9:23; Joshua24: 15). (1Timothy 5:8; Deuteronomy 6:6-9). God intends for husbands to maximize not only for the physical needs of their wife and family but also for the spiritual. This means that along with supplying food, shelter, clothing, etc., you are to make clear to your family all that the kingdom includes. You should be the primary source of Gospel teaching for your family, and you are to be instrumental to bringing each family member into salvation and the fullness of the Spirit. Just as Jesus did, you are to give godly purpose to the lives of your wife and family. In giving counsel and direction, always keep in mind the spiritual purpose in the situation (Luke 9:10- 17, 12:32, 5:8- 10, 4:31.32 We must be - Example of God's Heart (Mark 10:44; Matthew 6:14,15; Mark 16:17.18). God's heart is always for reconciliation and restoration inclusive of family's weakness and healing. Having the ability to be quick and constant in forgiveness and repentance, while serving wife and family with a humble spirit and a joyful heart, knowing that Jesus forgave before He was asked.

The polarity of the wife's role.

The wife reflection of God's Creativity (1 Cor.12:7; Titus 2:3-5). Proverbs 31:13-27. God has placed within each woman unique talents and gifts. Husbands, never compare your wife to others but allow God to develop what's uniquely for you. Know who she is in Christ and be confident in your love for her. She reflects specific aspect of God's personality, and ministry flowing from her will reveal the aspect of God gift in her. Your gifts and talents complement and complete each other. As a couple you should be in harmony in your flow even if you are working or ministering separately (Matthew 28:18-20; 1 Corinthians 12:25).

Husbands, loving your wife as Jesus loves the Church means being sensitive to her needs- spirit, soul, and body. Supporting your wife when the Spirit tells you she needs comforting, not when you think she needs comforting. Minister to her from the word. Jesus responded to His Church with empathy, not sympathy. It' is important for wives to know that they are "covered" by their husbands. Do not abdicate your protection over her or cause her to feel abandoned and alone. Be a gentle, steadfast unmovable man of God, allowing your physical love to minister to her needs (Mark 6:34; Luke 12:35- 48). Husbands, like Jesus, must take a firm, uncompromising stand against sin even when it might be easier to look the other way; as disciplinarians, hating the sin but loving the sinner. You must keep your family on track in their relationship with the Lord, pointing out to them areas of deficiency that need to be corrected. Exhortation, however. must always be mixed with love and encouragement. Never crush with your words, but edify and lift, even when challenging to excellence. Remember, you must honor and respect your authority to be respected (Luke 19:45, 20:45-47; Luke 20:20-26). Even more importantly, be not deceived: God cannot be mocked. A man reaps what he sows,' the one who sows to please his sinful nature, from that nature will reap destruction; the one who sows to please the Spirit, from the Spirit will reap eternal life. Let us not become weary in doing good, for at the proper time we will reap a harvest if we do not give-up" (Galatians 6:7-9 NIV).

The spiritual laws, just like natural laws, are destined by God to fulfill that for which they are created. Ignorance of the law does not stop it from operating. If someone jumps from a fifth-story window and does not know about the law of gravity, their lack of knowledge will not keep them from falling. This truly would be a case of someone perishing for lack of knowledge (Hosea 4:6). We walk every day in the effects of spiritual laws. We may be ignorant of their operation, but nevertheless, these laws operate and determine the outcome. One of the most basic of these laws is sowing and reaping. This law, as described in Galatians 6:7-9, indicates that we are going to reap a harvest; it is inevitable a sure thing. It further explains that this harvest is going to be a direct result of what we have planted. It matters not that we know if we are planting or not. We reap what we sow.

FIRST LIGHT

The sun came up and the night
blanket has rolled away.
The stars have retreated giving way
to the day. May the sunshine in your path today.
May the breeze be gentle in every way.
May the clouds be beautiful and silver
in a very special way.
May the sunset be glorious each and
Every day.

93

Chapter 15

The Intermittent Touch in Strife

We live in times of polarization and fragmentation. In many places, the ties that have historically bound societies together  have come apart. Our homes, churches and families are brewing with a strong and growing distrust of everything under the sun. We don't trust many things let alone our elected leaders and government officials. We don't have high confidence in our healthcare. Our suspicions concerning the church have not been immune to our cynicism. We have even approached the bride of Christ with wariness and uncertainty. All this fear is exacerbated by social media, which amplifies our distrust and rewards our outrage. As a result, many of us are less happy, less trusting, and angrier than ever. Division and angst have become like oxygen. News flash…. The scriptures said it was going to happen. We can feel and are experiencing the demise, like a sandcastle at high tide. For where envying and strife is, there is confusion and every evil work "(James 3:16 KJV). It is now the hour for a man to cease from strife and keep aloof from it (Proverbs 20:3a AMP). We must take an active stand against strife. The painful polarity in the body of Christ has not been immune to the polarization. Our congregations have had to navigate higher levels of conflict, controversy, and contentiousness. The pain of divisions is disheartening. Yet… here we are, the blood-bought people of God, united by Christ, but divided over so much else. This situation has some of us wishing we were still arguing over whether to sing contemporary worship songs or what color carpet to lay in the sanctuary. As a Christian it was disheartening to witness all the strife in the church today. It's good to be reminded that polarization in the church is not new. In fact, it's a problem as old as the church. Already in Acts 6, the Greek-speaking Jews complained that their widows were being neglected (Acts 6:1). Paul admonishes another church for its divisions, quarreling, jealousy, and strife (1 Corinthians 1:10–11; 3:4). They found superiority in their allegiances to either Paul, or Apollos, or Peter, forgetting that Christ is all in all.

Consequentially… Again and again, through Scripture and church history, when sinful people consistently gather, they consistently sin against one another and eventually turn on one another. Strife is very much like a merry-go-round. Is easier to stop when first spun than when is going full speed (Proverbs 15:1). It's more important to avoid strife than to appear justified (Matthew 23:12). The polarity of Paradox of Christ, as described in Hebrews tells us to cast off our sin that clings so closely, and instead look to Jesus, "the founder and perfecter of our faith" (Hebrews 12:1–2). By looking to Jesus, and his paradoxical qualities, we find help to navigate our polarized age. Jesus doesn't fit into any of our neat and tidy categories or tribes. He is pro-justice, pro-mercy, and pro-life. Jesus is gentle and lowly in heart, and he also will return to make war against his enemies. He is the meekest man that ever walked on earth, yet he will strike down the rebellious nations and tread the winepress of God's wrath (Revelation 19:11–15). He will save to the utmost with unparalleled grace and mercy, and he will rule with a rod of iron.

The Polarity of Difference always lead us where we need to go in Christ. We do not typically, gravitate to the ways of Jesus Christ; we align with those excellencies more natural to our personality and wiring. Who He is, however, admonishes us all to not be one-sided or one-dimensional. Jesus's example and teaching cuts both ways, admonishing us and encouraging each of us to be more Christlike than we are. For example, tender believers may be quick to revel in the compassion of

Christ: "Come to me, all who labor and are heavy laden, and I will give you rest" (Matthew 11:28). They may resonate deeply with Jesus's weeping outside Lazarus's tomb (John 11:35). Meanwhile, zealous-for-truth believers might admire his woes to the Pharisees. They may resonate more with Jesus's rebuke of Peter: "Get behind me, Satan!" (Matthew 16:23). Those of us who are naturally inclined toward compassion and sympathy need to learn from his courageous conviction. We need to beware of minimizing the whole counsel of God to avoid hurting someone's feelings or drawing harsh criticism. We will want to unashamedly portray the truth of Christ accurately, as we comfort and care for hurting people. And we might be slow to condemn those contending for truth in the public square who don't do it exactly the way we would.

The gospel will necessarily offend some, and standing for truth in a world set against the truth will require courage and boldness and may even appear quarrelsome in some eyes. The same is true for those who speak the truth more freely. Some of us are quite gifted at saying the hard things but need to grow in doing so with love. If we can speak with the tongues of men and angels, but have not love, we are noisy gongs and clanging cymbals (1 Corinthians 13:1). We will pray for greater compassion and sympathy, being quick to listen and weep with those who weep. Proverbs remind us, "A soft answer turns away wrath, but a harsh word stirs up anger" (Proverbs 15:1). Do our words, and the hearts behind those words, consistently reflect the priorities of Christ? We want to become the kind of paradox that we treasure and follow in Jesus. As you study Christ, watch where you lean and where you lean away, and then deliberately lean into the diverse excellencies of Christ. Find courage in his example. Where you are prone to wander, work to realign yourself more and more with the direction of scripture. Only the Power of God can change a pattern of strife in a relationship.

Ponder this....

We look for signs of true repentance in our brother or sister (husband or wife) before we are willing in words and action to release them from their guilt. If those signs are not there, we often remind them of their need to repent. Even if we keep our mouths shut, our hearts betray us for they are filled with self-righteous indignation. We are quick to find fault with the one we have not forgiven. To forgive means to grant free pardon for or remission of an offense or debt; to give up all claims. Jesus purchased forgiveness for us, and God freely grants us pardon. The full price for forgiveness has been paid. We are not to charge others or extract the payment we desire before we forgive. Jesus directed us to forgive each other in the same way that we want God to forgive us. Matthew :14.15 in the amplified version reads, "For if you forgive people their trespasses that is, their reckless and willful sins, leaving them letting them go and giving up resentment your heavenly Father will also forgive you. But if you do not forgive others their trespasses their reckless and willful sins, leaving them, letting them go and giving up resentment neither will your father forgive you your trespasses." God has set the standard. We can only be forgiven as we forgive. Very often, however, we are like the unmerciful servant in Matthew 18:23-35. We seek to be totally forgiven by God and have the slate wiped clean regarding our sins, but we can readily justify holding on to the sins of others. It is the desire of our Father's heart that we learn to release all claim to offenses and allow each other the same peace that we seek to obtain from Him. The unmerciful servant who refused to forgive as he had been forgiven was turned over to the torturers. The polarity of Matthew 18:35 says, 'This is how my heavenly Father will treat each of you unless you forgive your brother from your heart." Very often unforgiveness manifests in physical and mental illness. It is often the root of demonic strongholds. The one refusing to forgive is affected as much as the one not forgiven.

Chapter 16

Intermittent Touch of Prayer

What is it about prayer, or what is the power of prayer that would cause the disciples to want to learn how to do it  correctly? A basic definition of the power prayer is when you invite heaven's resources to intervene in your earthly situation. Since heaven's resources are unlimited, then you are inviting the omnipotent God into the equation and asking him to fix or do something about your circumstance. When you grasp that, then you are getting ahold of what the power of prayer is. This is where I really had to discern the intention of what was in my heart. It wasn't until I honestly looked in the mirror and saw who I was portraying. We all wear masks, we just don't want to face the reality of our pains, suffering, and social pressure, consequently we hide behind our mask in prayer. Wanting more but not able to discern which way to proceed or what to ask for. There are numerous scriptures throughout the bible that encourage us to pray and highlight the true power that is in prayer, for instance these two verses and so many others, you can see that one of the powers in prayer is when God's people ask for his help in their current situation, we pray all the times. The Hebrew word itself contains a range of meaning. "Executing judgment" (Ex,21:22) or thinking (Gen,48:11) to pray, may also refer to a process of accounting or contemplation. The root word prayer is a derivative of the Latin word "precari" which means "to be," It's important to reference the Hebrew word, "tefilah" along with its root "pele;" which means, the act of self-analysis or self-evaluation. Gooden further evaluates that when he was touched that his focus no-longer included others, however it was private. Not that it could not include other, but its focus had to be on self. It was here the revelation of "your will be done and not my own". This had to reflect the essential aspect to prayer: confession, petition, intercession, thanksgiving, and praise. Prayer must be sincere and with the right motives. The word of God says the effectual fervent prayer of a righteous man avail much. What is the effectual fervent prayer of a righteous man? The noticeable difference when you have been touched, your prayers will be cultivated in humility, and acceptance thus establishing your relationship with the God in the right manner. Akin to a baby cradled in his mother's arms.

Gooden says he cannot explain it, you must experience it. When we commit our ways to Christ the spirit of God will intercede on our behalf when we do not know what to pray for. We understand that… "the effectual fervent prayer of a righteous man availed much,' and has great power that produces wonderful results" (NLT). I really came to understand the perplexity of event polarizing, when I positioned my life up with the polarity of differences, that is when I began recognizing, answered prayers and of things I didn't know I needed. The fervent prayer of the righteous is not in vain. The righteous man is nothing like the prophets of Baal who called upon Baal and prayed to him in vain, for Baal never heard them nor answered them. The God of the righteous is the only true God, He lives, and hears the prayer of the righteous when they call upon Him. Hence our confidence is that whatever we earnestly ask in prayer He hears us. We can find quite a lot of examples in the Bible that confirms that the prayer of the righteous is powerful and produces results. Perhaps 'the most important lesson of our walk in Christ as men and women is to have active prayer lives. The active prayer life will result in your most inner thoughts being revealed, and the more you communicate the more of what's in your heart comes out of your mouth. For out of the abundance of the heart, the mouth speaks. The condition of your heart will reveal your intentions, especially if it is seated in your own righteousness. Jesus told this parable: 'Two men went up to the temple to pray, one a Pharisee and the other a tax collector. The Pharisee stood by himself and prayed: 'God, I thank you that I am not like other people—robbers, evildoers, adulterers—or even like this tax collector. I fast twice a week and give a tenth of all I get. 'But the tax collector stood at a distance. He would not even look up to heaven, but beat his breast and said, 'God, have mercy on me, a sinner. 'I tell you that this man, rather than the other, went home justified before God. For all those who exalt themselves will be humbled, and those who humble themselves will be exalted' (Luke 18:9-14). There is a stark difference between these two men praying. One came with full confidence, knowing he had done everything right and his praying was just the icing on the cake of his self-righteousness. The other one could barely lift his eyes toward heaven, yet he is the one that experienced the power in prayer. There were two simple but important reasons why; if there is a key to experiencing power in prayer, it is making sure you pray from a place of reality. What I mean by this is that you don't hide the truth of your situation and how you feel about it, and the reason we never have real times of breakthrough in prayer is because we often approach God like the Pharisee, either falsely believing we have it all together or thinking we must get it together before we approach God, because "God helps those who help themselves." The truth is you need to come to God just the way you are, bring the situation just the way it is and be open, real, and honest before God. This is what God wants from you and when you do this, you position yourself to experience the real power in prayer. It may take time; let it. I mentioned God helping those who help themselves. The truth is the opposite. God helps those who realize they can't help themselves, those who cry out to him for his help. When you invite heaven's resources into your situation, that means you are acknowledging that; you alone are not enough. As

100

powerful as prayer is, there is one thing that prayer, faith, or anything else can't do. Prayer cannot supersede or override the  will of God. You can pray as much as you want, for as long as you want, and with as much faith as you can muster, but it will not change what God has willed to do. For this reason, one of the most powerful weapons in prayer is agreement with God's will. Not only are we encouraged to pray God's will be done (think the Lord's prayer) we are also assured that when we pray according to God's will, he will acknowledge what we are praying for.

This is the confidence we have in approaching God: that if we ask anything according to his will, he hears us. And if we know that he hears us, whatever we ask, we know that we have what we asked of him" (1 John 5:14-15). As great as the spiritual benefits are from prayer, there have been studies that show there are physical ones as well. Admittedly this is not my area of expertise, but here is information from a 2009 study by Koenig and colleagues, that found that, "six weekly in-person Christian prayer sessions with patients at a primary care office lowered their depression and anxiety symptoms and increased their optimism." Because God understands fully all the benefits of prayer, it is no surprise that he would encourage us to do it. It is why verses like this make more sense. "Cast all your anxiety on him because he cares for you" (1 Peter 5:7). As these patients continued in prayer, their anxieties and worries were lowered. This happens because in prayer, they transferred their anxieties from themselves to God and allowed Him to carry them. In prayer God is not just concerned about your need, He is concerned about you as well. Part of the reason God desires you to pray is because he knows it is good for your health. The things you let go of and give to God are not only good for your spirit, but they are also good for your body and mind too. This is a power of prayer that we most certainly overlook. One of the most intimate, essential to our health is prayer; but it intermittently takes dedication, practice, and consistency. When you enter prayer, these important guidelines can keep us out of conflicts. First, prayer time should begin with praise and worship of our Lord. The Word tells us to enter the presence of the Lord with praise (Psalm 100:4), and that the Lord inhabits the praises of His people (Psalm 22:3). Repeatedly throughout scripture we are instructed to praise the Lord. Praise and worship do not need to be a formalized program. We have become conditioned that praise and worship must be led by a team and follow a certain order. Just begin to praise and worship the Lord from your heart and allow the Holy Spirit to teach you. You will be greatly blessed as you enter His presence. Prayer will flow out of praise. Additionally, when praying, follow the instruction of the Apostle Paul, "Do not fret or have any anxiety about anything, but in every circumstance and in everything by prayer and petition [definite requests] with thanksgiving continue to make your wants known to God" (Philippians 4:6 Amplified). The Word says to present a petition, a written request. If you write down your requests, you can keep track of them and keep a record of answered prayers. Date your requests and then document the answers you receive. This orderly record of your prayer time will be a great encouragement to you as you see how mighty God has been on your behalf. It is also very important that prayer be limited to those things which are of mutual concern, rather you are single or married, however to both husband and wife. Individual prayer time should be used for those strictly personal concerns such as countries, causes, or specific people for which God has burdened us to pray. Joint payer-time should focus on those people or situations that you are interceding together for. Discuss what these things will be before you enter prayer. It is not difficult to find mutual prayer concerns. Do not concentrate on the ones you are not burdened with together or criticize your spouse for not wanting to pray for what concerns you. Instead, concentrate on the ones you hold in common. James 4:2,3 make very clear what is achieved in this manner: "You want something but don't get it. You kill and covet, but you cannot have what you want. You quarrel and fight. You do not have, because you do not ask God. When you ask, you do not receive because you ask with wrong motives, that you may spend what you get on your pleasures" (NIV). Matthew 18:19 describes the value of agreement. "Again, I tell you, if two of you on earth agree (harmonize together, together make a symphony) about anything and everything, whatever they shall ask, it will come to pass and be done for them by My Father in heaven" (Amplified). Often Christians use this scripture to "lock" God into doing what they desire. The concern here is that each sought his or her own way. Each was willing to compromise, battle, or manipulate to achieve that, which was felt to be the correct decision. The process of agreement usually involves bringing our spouse over to our way of thinking or going over to theirs. The perplexity of event in this polarity, in either case, one had to conform to the other to agree. Matthew 18:19, however, speaks of harmonizing, making a symphony; simultaneously combining tones. In an orchestra there are many instruments, each making a unique sound. The goal of the symphony is not to make them alike but to blend their uniqueness into one beautiful music. Clearly God's plan for agreement is different than ours. To reach agreement; each must examine the polarity of differences; and align their goals as one, walking in agreement, thus fulfilling the will of Christ in their lives.

Jesus set the example for us when He lived His earthly life. He always sought to fulfill the will of His Father: "...I seek not mine own will, but the will of the Father who hath sent me" (John 5:30 KJV); and "My food... .is to do the will of him who sent me and to finish his work" (John 4:34 NIV). Our Father has a will for everything we, His children, do. We need to learn to begin seeking that will in all things instead of pursuing our own desires. We also have assurance from scripture that agreement based on the will of God will come to pass; this is the confidence we have in approaching God; that if we ask anything according to His will, He hears us. (1 John 5:14,15  NIV). It is within this mindset, that I'm reminded of the words of Paul, when I was a child, I spoke as a child but when I became a man, I put away childish things. Thus, I had to lay aside the weight and the sins that so easily were besetting me, from maturing and not fulfilling my role as husband. I could no longer deny my posture (Ephesians 5:23), realizing, I am responsible to God and that provides added counsel and confirmation. Proverbs 11:14; Proverbs 15:22 (Amplified). The paradox of not allowing circumstances, imposed to pressure or sway me away from His word, while seeking God's heart. This revelation along with the polarity of differences helped us to understand that some prayers will be delayed or not answered. The enemy delayed the answer to Daniel for 21 days (Daniel10). Learning to accept, your will be done on earth as it is in heaven will always give us strength by the Spirit of God. The waiting assures the process which makes it possible to proceed in confidence. That agreement enables His will to come to pass on the earth. Moreover, the husband, in his role of headship, must declare that he and his wife will not take any action on a matter without genuine, heartfelt agreement. This does not deny the headship of the husband (Ephesians 5 :23). It enhances it with the added dimension of counsel and confirmation (Proverbs 11:14). After all, even the word must confirm itself. We cannot take one isolated scripture and build a case on it if we cannot find confirming scriptures elsewhere. Why should we then think that we as humans need no confirmation? The husband is still responsible to God for the direction his family takes. By achieving agreement this way, however, he also has the protection of confirming prayer. Do not allow circumstances imposed from outside your relationship to pressure or sway you from seeking God's perfect will for you. God knows your time frame and will give you the answer in His timing. Do not allow deadlines set by man to be your criteria for decision. If, by your own admission, you are willing to proceed without agreement, the enemy will delay the answer the same way he did with Daniel. No deadline is a deadline unless God says it is. Refuse second best. Always go for true, heartfelt agreement given by the Spirit of God. Thereupon, God created man in his own image, in the image of God created he him; male and female created he them. And God blessed them, and God said unto them, be fruitful and multiply, and replenish the earth, and subdue it..." (Genesis 1:27,28 KJV).

MY CHILD

For you my child, I suffered and
died and rose from dead. Hung there I did just
For you. So, you would know, I'd always be true.
These words I say to you, may they bring
you closer each day.
Remember my child, my love for you will
never fade away. Remember, what I had to
give; I gave at Calvary.
What I want is for you to be happy and free.
What I felt was tears and pain.
What I've seen is a world waiting to be set free.
Just give it all to me.

Chapter 17

Intermittent Intimacy

Upon hearing these words, you probably immediately jumped to thinking about physical intimacy, but other forms of intimacy are just as important, especially when it comes to  romantic relationships. Let's look at some different forms of intimacy. However, before I do. I must admit…I knew nothing about intimacy before my transformation in Christ. How I looked at it was framed by my environment had nothing to do with what true intimacy was. I do not think I would have ever understood intimacy, if I had not first learned what love stood for. The polarity of differences within relationships sometimes seems that our two sets of needs directly oppose each other. The feeling that our needs are being challenged often leads to difficulties experiencing true intimacy. The paradox of uniting with other people to feel a part of a larger group or existence that connects us to other people on common ground. Intimacy; is therefore, being able to be and share our true selves with others. To be cared for and loved. This is easier said than done. I know because I never felt I could connect to anyone on a real level due to my past mental state. It took years of pain and suffering along with self-examinations. I had to crawl out of my own darkness; and into the other side of self-need of asserting my knowledge and abilities and to have control over my surroundings. To simply be and function as my own person independently. To be unique and to excel at accomplishments and allow my light to shine before the world to glorify Christ. The polarity of difference can sometimes appear in direct conflict, they however can exist harmoniously together if we recognize the equal importance of all things. Similarly, when needs are off balance, we can feel unhappy, frustrated, and disappointed with ourselves. When there is too much weight on one need it takes away from another need. For example, if you spend all your time working to fulfill your need for distinctiveness, you may find yourself feeling lonely due to the lack of intimacy. Then, when you try to enter a relationship, you feel that the attention needed is taking away from your ability to focus on your work. Your partner complains that you don't spend enough time together. So, you end the relationship. However, a more purposeful approach would be to create a system where both needs are met within boundaries. Also, understanding why you are more strongly motivated to work than to be cared for. Perhaps you have difficulty trusting intimacy, because you feel achievements are easier to control and less risk free in getting satisfaction? Or perhaps you were raised in an environment where success was encouraged but outward expressions of emotions were discouraged? Perhaps you always felt that no matter what you did, unless you worked hard and were the best at it, you would never be good enough to live up to your parents' expectations? I encourage you to reflect on instances when one needs to challenge another and then decide if it is being challenged by others today or if you are repeating patterns of the past. Needs left unexamined will lead to a "come here/go away" pattern, where you want to be intimately close to your partner but your self needs, or relational needs feel threatened. Once you can better understand how your views developed, you will be in a better position to recognize when they are interfering with experiencing true intimacy in your life. Additionally, true emotional intimacy can be one of the most critical factors of all relationships. It is characterized by being able to share your deepest, most personal feelings with another person. When people experience this type of intimacy, they feel safe and secure enough to share and know that they will be understood, affirmed, and cared for. Isn't this the attribute of Christ, allowing us to lay all things upon Him because He cares. This design cannot be duplicated by Satan's counterfeits, it cannot be produced through ungodly means. Satan has falsely promised all kinds of avenues into intimacy with God. Religions, communing with nature, meditation, etc. Every one of them misses the vital element of covenant relationships. Spiritual purity is required for spiritual intimacy, and this is only available through the shed blood of Jesus (Hebrews 9:22); which provides the only means to intimacy with God. This Intimacy is essential in all relationship because it forms a basis for connection and communication. It ensures that each person feels understood, allows them to be themselves, and ensures that each person gets the care and comfort that they need. In the context of matrimonial intimacy, research has found couples that were in long-term romantic relationships, experience more emotional intimacy and experience higher levels of sexual desire and sexual activity, thus experiencing more satisfaction within their relationship. The cause-and-effect lead to better physical well-being and improved mental health. Having close, intimate relationships is also pivotal for our wellbeing. It can also combat feelings of loneliness and help people better manage the stress they experience in life. While Intimacy is a Holy Covenant within marriage and the basis for intimacy between man and woman. The commitment and protection of covenant allows a couple to be totally vulnerable to each other. They will experience a depth in relationship possible only under covenant covering (Genesis 2:24). The man and woman are designed both physically and emotionally to experience great pleasure and satisfaction from sexual union. Sex should be the most fulfilling physical experience on earth when it is under covenant covering. The Song of Solomon references the fruit, gardens, and vineyards are used in conjunction with the relationship between the lover and his beloved. Sexual union as God created it is not self-centered nor self-seeking. It is refreshing and energizing. Take time to read Song of Solomon as husband and wife and let it reveal the beauty of sexual union as God created.

Consequently, the downside to this, is sin, and because of it, many are not able to experience sexual intimacy as God intends  because of sexual sin. Just as Satan fabricated spiritual counterfeits to imitate spiritual intimacy, he has also fabricated sexual counterfeits to imitate sexual intimacy. Instead of producing sexual intimacy, they are damaging counterfeit. (Romans 1:24-27). Our own inability to accept the covenant of intimacy, strips the ability to be intimate. Instead of edifying and ministering, it degrades and defiles, makes foul, dirty, or unclean; pollutes, taints, and violates the chastity of sexual union. Instead of enhancing, it diminishes (Proverbs 6:32,33). No wonder scripture tells us that one who commits sexual sin, sins against his own body (1 Corinthians 6:18). The paradox union of intimacy reveals man was created to be tender toward and understanding of his wife (1 Peter 3:7) Jesus is the example of the intimate husband. His overwhelming love of His bride. A calloused man operating outside of true intimacy, will manifest a hardened heart in lust, not love, towards his wife. A man with a hardened heart cannot love a woman the way God intends. He can only show affection or interest in her when he wants to have sex. Once a man has hardened his heart in sexual sin, only God can soften it again (Ezekiel 36:26). When men grab hold of this, they will understand; a wife was created to respond to the love of the man to whom she is married (Ephesians 5:22). In response to his love, she gives herself totally to her husband. He loves and enhances that which she has entrusted to him, and she responds again with greater love. A woman who is cherished usually has no problem loving and giving in return. This is evident in the Song of Solomon, which makes it clear that intimacy, as God intends it, produces life, with references to fruit, gardens, and vineyards contained throughout the Song of Solomon, which are used in conjunction with relationships between the lover and his beloved. Sexual union, as God created it, is not a self-centered, self-seeking relationship. It never fulfills self at the expense of the other. Sexual love according to God's plan is refreshing and energizing, always desiring to give more than it receives. In the creation of children, God has given us a natural example of the life-giving potential of our sexual union (Gen.1:28; Mal 2:15). Read the Song of Solomon together and you will begin to see the beauty of sexual union as God created it. Just as sexual intimacy was God's gift to Adam and Eve in the garden (Genesis 1 :28, 31), it is His wedding gift to each couple that enters His covenant plan of marriage (1 Cor 7:3-5). In contrast many, are not able to experience sexual intimacy as God intends, due to the deceiving people into believing that masturbation, homosexuality, fornication, adultery, incest, and other sexual perversions produce sexual intimacy. In this case they are damaging counterfeits (Romans 1:24-27). The demise of not acknowledging and seeking help will almost always result in wounding from seeking fulfillment in compulsive behaviors linking to, and in alcohol, drugs, food, gambling, or shopping. Each time the disappointment is greater, and fulfillment slips farther away (Proverbs 14:12). Spiritual purity is the basis for spiritual intimacy, so sexual purity is the basis for sexual intimacy. In conclusion, if you have lost that purity, Jesus longs to restore it to you. If you entered marriage sexually pure, your sexual intimacy should be able to deepen as the years go by. The paradox of purity is sometimes maintained through fear or distrust of intimacy. Justification of sin only perpetuates the consequences. If you are not sure if something was sin or if scripture does not specifically mention it, ask the following questions: Did it edify? Did one or both partners feel defiled? Was there disagreement whether it was right or not? The polarity of difference demands we forgive them and release all things to Christ Jesus. Forgive yourself, whether you were a willing partner or an innocent victim. Forgive yourself for the defilement. Begin to love yourself as Jesus loves you. You are precious to Him, therefore discontinue all soul ties that were established by previous sexual activities. When the mind, will, and emotions are deeply involved in a relationship, soul ties are formed. Soul ties hold us mentally and emotionally to previous relationships and people (1 Samuel 18:1) If the relationship is not godly, the hold is ungodly. It keeps us from being healed. (Genesis 34:2,3,8).

Break all soul ties with all people with whom you have engaged in sexual activity.

However, discontinuing soul ties does not necessarily mean ending the relationship. You can continue to relate, for example, to a previous spouse due to children. The emotional and mental ties will be broken. Take authority over demonic spirits given access through sin. They create areas of demonic hold. To maintain your victory and obtain total healing, you must keep yourself from impurity and renew your mind with the word of God (Romans 12:1,2). Your mind is the battle ground in which the enemy is going to attempt to regain what he has lost. Therefore, guard yourselves from the worldly image of sexual lust fed through pornography, soap operas, romance novels, etc. Refuse the worldly message. The word intimacy is derived from the Latin word "intimus," which means 'inner' or 'innermost'. In most romance languages, the word for intimate refers to a person's innermost qualities. Intimacy allows people to bond with each other on many levels. Therefore, it is a necessary component of healthy relationships. I want to admonish you to renew your mind (replace the old thought patterns) with the mind of Christ (1 Corinthians 2:16). Lock your shields of faith together for protection against the enemy. if one spouse was a victim of incest or rape, give permission to share when shame is trying to come upon them. Guard your sexual union together as husband and wife. For this reason, God created a man to be tender and understanding toward the woman he marries (1 Peter 3:7). Jesus is the example of the intimate Husband. His overwhelming love for His bride makes it easy for us to respond lovingly to Him. When a man sins sexually, his heart  becomes hardened. The tender, loving heart that was God's plan for him cannot endure the ravages of sexual sin. A man with a hardened heart cannot love a woman the way God intends. Many times, in marriage a man's callused and hardened heart manifests in lust, not love, towards his wife. The man is unable to show affection or interest in his wife other than when he wants to have sex. When he looks at her or touches her, she feels defiled and doesn't know why. Once a man has hardened his heart, only God can soften it again (Ezekiel 36:26). The counterfeit of Satan will never enable him to love as God intended. Many times, in marriage this manifests insecurity and a poor self-image. A wife may not be able to respond to her husband physically because of the hardened heart to intimacy, so she continually expects her husband to fulfill her. The deep inner emptiness manifests mentally, in he doesn't love me. The truth is that only Jesus can fill that void and give her the peace and fulfillment she desires. Men and women who have been wounded may seek fulfillment in compulsive behaviors such as drugs, alcohol, food, gambling, or shopping, or one sexual partner after another. Each time, however, the disappointment is greater and the fulfillment they are seeking slips farther away (Proverbs 14:12).

This means there is hope! God, who designed sexual intimacy, has redeemed us from the curse of sin and death (Romans 8:2). You can tell how important a matter is to the heart of God by how much time the enemy spends perverting it. Satan has spent a great deal of time counterfeiting the intimacy of sexual union. God, however, desires so much for us to know true intimacy that He has provided a way of healing when we have missed the mark. Your Sexual Union is much more than an act. Be led of the Spirit in all things (Romans

8:14), including your sexual union. Strive to have intimacy not lust, you cannot overcome it alone. You need the help of your spouse. First receive the deliverance and cleansing of the blood of Jesus. Then join in one-flesh unity against these demonic strongholds. Become accountable to each other in areas of weakness. Remember, though, you are not your spouse's Holy Spirit. It is your job to intercede and to stand beside and support. Allow the conviction of sin to come from the One who does it best. The devil has used these tools to divide you in the past. Now join in the power of Jesus against him and his forces of darkness. Together you will have the victory!

Consider the scripture, "Drink water from your own cistern, running water from your own well. Should your springs overflow in the streets, your streams of water in public places? Let them be yours alone, never to be shared with strangers. May your fountain be blessed, and may you rejoice in the wife of your youth, A loving doe, a graceful deer - may her breasts satisfy you always, may you ever be captivated by her love..." (Proverbs 5: 1 5-20 NIV). (KJV) says, "For as he thinketh in his heart, so is he..." Our thoughts determine our actions. To deepen your sexual union, you need to concentrate on each other. Are either of you involved in pornography? Know for certain that there is no such thing as "innocent" pornography. Pornography comes from the same root word as "pomeria" in Ephesians 6:12, which means depravity or spiritual wickedness. It is one of the most deceptive strongholds of the enemy. Lust is never satisfied. A thought today will be an action tomorrow. If the enemy cannot keep you from entering the intimacy of God's covenant plan, marriage, he will attempt to make you compromise that covenant commitment. He tells you his counterfeits will bring excitement to your sexual union with your spouse, but he knows they will rob you of intimacy with each other.

The polarity of differences in intimacy influences your children. We must not convey to them that sex is bad to keep them out of sin. This will certainly rob them of the joy God intends for them in marriage. Teach them honestly regarding the fulfillment of sexual intimacy along with the reasons for God's commandments. They will be better equipped to enter marriage pure and with a healthy attitude toward sex. The wounding of sexual sin need not be repeated in the next generation. Wisdom and knowledge of the word of God will prepare them and our obedience will be their example. To further enable you as a couple to incorporate wisdom into your daily life. Know that your walk is meant to be lived together, therefore studying together is a MUST in lieu of your individual walk with Christ. Work together. The polarity of difference in each experience enables you to delve deeply into the paradox of Christ, not merely skim the surface as you prefer. You will receive as much from the relationship as you are willing to put into it. You set the pace and receive as you choose. Be honest with each other and with God, you will be blessed beyond your expectations. You only get what you put into it.

THIS TOO WILL PASS

Alive but dead, alone in my stead.
The air that I breathe from whence.
It comes, I cannot conceive.
The sun, the moon, the stars shine bright
Yet in my heart there's only night.
Why can't life be better for me why don't I hear the bluebird sing?
My day will come…It will come. My light shall shine and all that I am will be found.
This too will pass.

Chapter 18

Intermittent Deception

In Corinthians 7:7, the Apostle Paul recommends that, to avoid fornication, every man should be allowed to have his  own wife, and every woman her own husband: But I speak this by permission, and not of commandment. For I would that all men were even as I. But every man hath his proper gift of God, one after this manner, and another after that. I say therefore to the unmarried and widows, it is good for them if they abide even as I. But if they cannot contain it, let them marry for it is better to marry than to burn. Gooden says, he had to acknowledge his life was misguidance to what he thought was love was only lust and desire. Solomon is certainly against marriage. The fear of lust and its evils no doubt shaped Solomon's attitude towards women, and, through Solomon, the Church's attitude and society's attitude, or historical attitude. We must realize that lust is a strong and subversive force, and very difficult to resist. King David (Solomon's father) was undone by his lust for the bathing Bathsheba.

Furthermore, David was caught and entangled in lust. He sought forgiveness, repented but he still had to pay for his sins. You can be set free from the deception of this world's enticement. In our churches we have seen souls that have committed the sin of lust and have taken down our homes and communities in a whirlwind that symbolizes their lack of self-control. Gooden explain to no surprise, we are no match for the force of lust and therefore are a poor defense against lust. Lust, in the words of Shakespeare, is 'a waste of shame'. To hide that shame, many cultures magic up a male demon who lays upon sleepers to have sex with them. This incubus (and the less prevalent female equivalent, or succubus) is made to carry the blame for embarrassing nocturnal emissions, disturbing claims of adultery and abuse, and even unexplained children. Another response to the shame of lust, and much more prevalent in our culture, is to pass off lust as romantic love. In contrast to lust, love is respectable, even commendable. We look on approvingly at a pair holding hands or hugging, but we look around for the police if they start acting out their lust. Love is the acceptable face of lust, but the love that is lust in disguise is arguably even more perverse and destructive, and, in that sense, even more shameful, than the lust that knows its name. While lust is hasty, furtive, and deceitful, love is patient, measured, and constant. While lust is all about taking, love is all about sharing. While lust is all about consuming, love is all about making. Lust is a poor start on any basis. Of course, there is nothing wrong with sexual desire per se, and none of us would be here without it. Sexual desire is a life force, to be enjoyed and even celebrated. But as with wine, the problems start when it turns from servant into master. Uncontrolled lust is especially unattractive in the elderly, because, as the saying goes, there is no fool like an old fool. Lust is hard to extinguish but can more readily be redirected. If Travis is angry at his boss, he may go home and act out his anger by smashing some plates, or he may instead run it off on a treadmill. This second instance of displacement, running off on the treadmill, is an example of sublimation, which is the channeling of unproductive or destructive forces into socially condoned and often constructive activities.

The deceiving devices of pornography and other sexual sins are rampant in our culture and in the church and almost accepted as the norm. Many have concluded that such behavior or at least the lust that drives them is fundamentally an unsolvable problem, a sin that will not be defeated in the lives of God's children. But this response is unacceptable in the face of the severe and incalculable damage that lust inflicts upon lives, families, and fellowships. If you want to overcome lust, you need to recognize what you are dealing with. A good place to start is to understand the "sexual desire"—the electric feeling of pleasure that has sex so enjoyable. Psychobiologic sexual desire involves our emotions, our bodies, and our cognitive functions. God designed these feelings for good. Sexual emotion occupies an essential role as an early phase of intimacy within the sexual union of marriage. Without it, we would not become aroused, and sex probably would not happen enough to keep reproduction going or marital ties binding. Sexual desire is only appropriate inside the marriage relationship. When we misuse this capacity—allowing ourselves an illicit sexual desire—it is sinful lust. Consider the following definition to understand this. Sexual lust is willfully allowing pleasurable gratification of wrongfully directed sexual desire that takes place deep inside. In short …It is something we choose to do. It is not forced upon us. Giving in to it may be driven by habit and undertaken without deliberation, but it is still a choice on our part. We enjoy it. The illicit sexual desire is intensely enjoyable in a way we cannot fully understand. God designed us so that even when we are merely looking to enjoy legitimate sexual pleasure, looking to lust, or contemplating sexual activity, we can realize a pleasurable sexual desire. We recognize when it happens because something clicks into place. We may claim that we are "doing nothing" and may be able to fool others, but we should not try to fool ourselves. God is not fooled. We are focusing our attention on a way that is not right. Sexual desire is only proper when it is grounded within a marriage relationship. This is hard to accept when we are in bondage to lust. We look for a way to justify our waywardly pointed gratification of sexual desire to convince ourselves that it is okay to let them roam. We cannot fully understand how sexual desire takes place. Our psychobiologic response is deep-seated and intensely personal. It occurs quickly and unmistakably,

117

long before (and oftentimes without any) externally visible evidence. This is, admittedly, a rather complicated definition. Jesus the Master craftsmen distilled all these elements into a phrase that instantly rings true. He termed what takes place when we sin this way "adultery in the heart" (Matthew 5:28). In doing so, he included all the above elements with an elegant, penetrating simplicity that a Christian cannot dismiss from his conscience.

Distinguishing Sexual Desire from Lust

There are a few objections that arise immediately in some who hear this explanation for the first time, and it's best to introduce them right from the start. The first objection is the assertion that the sexual desire which develops in a mostly indiscriminate way is nothing more than natural sexual desire. In fact, most definitions of lust describe it as a normal desire that has gone astray, without explaining plainly when this occurs. Unfortunately, there is a fundamental problem with using the term "desire" or "sexual desire" as the starting point when developing a suitable, practical definition of lust. The word "desire" conveys the idea of hope or wish for future fulfillment. In contrast, those who lust is not just thirsty, they are drinking from the cup as well. We are constantly exposed to sexual stimulations, primarily visual. This is the world in which we live. It is natural to have a sexual reaction to such stimulation. This is because sexual desire is a part of who we are. Thus, we are not permitted, however, to take the next step in cases when this sexual attraction is misdirected. Some may argue that one cannot stop illicit gratification. But there's an easy way to prove that wrong: we routinely recoil from lust or sexualized interactions with family members such as daughters or sisters. Focusing our attention to obtain an illicit sexual desire is willful and sinful. That quick gulp of sweet "stolen water" (Proverbs 9:17) is when we have crossed into sinful lust. We may want to minimize the adultery we are allowing in our hearts, but God does not. There is nothing wrong with sexual desire—if it is not followed up with lust. It is a finely tuned and powerful God-given capacity, and we should not expect it to go away or find any fault with it. God created the pleasures in the Garden of Eden: The issue is whether we will use our desires to engage in sin. Sexual desires are only permitted as we share and enjoy them within the marriage relationship. The sin of lust occurs when we allow ourselves illicit sexual pleasure by misusing sexual desire. Do not believe the lie that you cannot deny yourself illicit gratification when tempted. We can and must whenever we are tempted to sin.

Victory and freedom are focusing on the real problem, we can no longer sweep this under the rug and expect it to just go away in time. There is no time, it's now. -no-other-way. Recognizing that sexual desires and thoughts by themselves are not necessarily bound up with lust; but provides the key to overcoming it. Many attempt to eliminate their sexual desires and thoughts because they have habitually harnessed these to realize an illicit sexual desire. This approach is called "thought suppression." Thought suppression has been studied extensively and is best illustrated by the experiment of trying to stop oneself from thinking about a pink elephant. Unfortunately, this strategy has never proven to be effective. Instead, we need to accept that we will at times give rise to bad thoughts and will also continue to feel sexual desire in ways that we do not choose. Instead of suppressing our wayward thoughts and desires, we need to "bring them into captivity" (2 Corinthians 10:5) by denying them access to our hearts. The temptation to "go with it" must be resisted. Consequently, we are all born and shaped in iniquity. Let's be clear about this and we cannot shut down our desires and thoughts, nor should we seek to. The polarity of this is not the real problem. Simply

119

put…we must also recognize and repent whenever we misuse our desires or thoughts to accommodate sin and to develop practical strategies for gaining victory if we find ourselves being dominated by this sin. Many wrongly believe as I once did that sexual desires and sexual thoughts are parts of us that have special power. They feel that they have no choice when subjected to temptation but to allow these desires and thoughts to generate an illicit sexual desire. It has become an automatic response because they have crossed the line on a regular basis.

In conclusion…Paul concluded, do you not know that when you offer yourselves as obedient slaves, you are slaves to the one you obey, whether you are slaves to sin leading to death, or to obedience leading to righteousness? But thanks be to God that, though you once were slaves to sin, you wholeheartedly obeyed the form of teaching to which you were committed.… therefore, neither yield ye your members as instruments of unrighteousness unto sin: but yield yourselves unto God, as those that are alive from the dead, and your members as instruments of righteousness unto God. Joshua 24:15 However, our desires and thoughts do not force us to sin. Instead of slipping into sin, we need to act with the knowledge and confidence that God is faithful to provide "the way of escape" (1 Corinthians 10:13) whenever we are tempted. Entering that "way" necessarily means that we refuse to commit adultery within our hearts. Our focus needs to be on denying actual sin, growing to maturity as believers, and learning to please God. Our desires become evil when we act upon them by committing adultery in our hearts. By first putting to death our evil passions and desires, we can put on the new person and effectively abide in Christ. Allow Christ to touch you.

Chapter 19

Intermittent Victory

An architect knows that a solid foundation is essential to any building. Once the foundation is laid, supports are put in,  permitting the rest of the structure to be built. Jesus says... "I will show you what it's like when someone comes to me, listens to my teaching, and then follows it. It is like a person building a house who digs deep and lays the foundation on solid rock. When the floodwaters rise and come against that house, it stands firm because it is well built. Consequentially, anyone who hears and doesn't obey is like a person who builds a house right on the ground, without a foundation. Eventually the floods sweep down against that house, and collapses into a heap of ruins." Luke 6:47-49 (NLT). In Luke 6, Jesus explains the difference between a wise builder and a foolish one. A builder who is wise hears the word of God, applies it to his life, and as a result, stands firmly through turbulent times. However, because the foolish builder doesn't obey or apply God's principles and instructions, he's ruined when a raging storm hits his life. Gooden says, in this case, he finally came to the reality of what was vital to having a strong foundation, and that structure was in Christ. Besides, following God and submitting to his wisdom enables you to build a solid foundation based on spiritual values. As you base your life on him, there are a few areas you will need to continually focus on to cultivate a strong, healthy spiritual life. And this won't only benefit you; others will reap the blessings as well. Gooden suggest having a strong foundation is a step in the right direction to living your life for Christ. This foundation was established to withhold and anchor us all. On the other hand, a life lived after the carnality of this world will only yield the fruit of unrighteousness, sinking sand. The paradoxes of Christ, His tool for drawing us to a good foundation is essential to the integrity of the body/ building. The ability of a house to weather storms and the relentless power of decay is dependent on the quality of its foundation. Spiritually, Jesus Christ is the only foundation of the Christian faith. Salvation is the foundation of the Christian life, based upon the completed work of the cross; nothing else could be added to it. As a result, the fundamental tool for our foundation, faith, putting our trust in God through Christ became the integral tool to building a solid foundation. Thus, enabling us to face the storms, which inadvertently grounded us to remain as steady as a rock in our beliefs. Moreover, for this reason, it's wise to seek God daily and ask him to search your heart and make known what displeases him (Psalm 139:23-24). If you disobey him, your foundation will begin to crack. Consequentially, over time, as a Christian; I had fallen. Although I know I had the spirit from my repenting. There was still a lot I had to learn and grow into. The victory, however, isn't instant, as some communicate it is. This walk is intermittently being carved out to us. Listen to the wisdom Solomon's last words, "here is the conclusion of the matter". I further submit. It's important that you're planted in a local church where you can worship God, hear his word, and fellowship with other members of the body of Christ. In there, you'll grow and mature spiritually, as well as be able to use the spiritual gifts God has blessed you with. As a result, his Church will be nourished. (1Corinthians 14:12). In doing so, you will be taught how to be a good steward in your finances, which is a spiritual discipline that blesses your family. God is not pleased watching you living outside of your means, amassing material possessions, and accumulating irresponsible debt, which is unwise. When you manage your finances wisely, you eliminate needless stress (Mark 8:36). To elaborate on top of that, your body is God's living temple; his Spirit resides within you. When you harm your body, you're dishonoring God. Keeping your body healthy is a spiritual discipline that is part of the life God calls you to. Living a healthy lifestyle also permits you to carry out God's greater plans for your life (1 Corinthians 6:19-20).

I lived in total isolation from people in the church for a long time. Partly due to how and what I was learning. Additionally, what was being displayed before me was so contrary to scripture. It was bad enough that I had lost so much trust in our society, but to experience the same in the church was devastating. I had to learn through my own vises and accept that we all are living the same life at the same time, however experiencing God intermittently different. Therefore, the polarity of differences became more of me and you and not me or you. As a result, I embraced that all relationships are vital and should be cherished! The people in your life and your relationships with them are important to God, and they need to be valued and esteemed fittingly. God desires that you love others and seek to build them up, not tear them down. Also, knowing that bad company corrupts good character (1 Corinthians 15:33-34), be careful about whom you spend time with. I want to pause for a moment and elaborate on the paradox of victory, which does not come without a price, the victory we seek will only come at the end. Moreover, it's what many Christians want. It's what we've been promised by Christ himself. But several questions come to my mind, questions like: "Why don't we see more victory in Christ?" or "Why don't I have more victory in Christ myself?" I want to suggest that many Christians, in this generation have their conceptualization of Christianity fundamentally flawed."? For example, if we had been alive during the Crusades, most "good Christians" would have been certain that they could earn admission to heaven by going to fight in the Holy Land. All this to say, it is sometimes difficult to separate what God has told us is in truth from what we simply assume is true because everyone around us says or believes it is. At one point in time,

I assumed that "victory in Christ" or living a victorious Christian life in the middle of our sinful, messed-up world, meant having victory in my own life, as I chose to define it.  Because of my life growing up and the church culture as I knew it, I thought that having victory in Christ meant that I had to become increasingly self-sufficient. Living in America is a portrait for our independence, self-reliance, and willingness to "go it on our own." These qualities are tremendously helpful when homesteading or starting up a business, but they are not great assets when trying to find true victory in Christ. For me, this independent spirit has kept me spiritually stagnant.

In 1 John 5:34, we read, "This is love for God: to obey his commands. And his commands are not burdensome, for everyone born of God overcomes the world. This is the victory that has overcome the world, even our faith" (NIV). So, I believe that for me to become victorious, I need to grow in my love for and obedience to Christ. I want to be like Him…He was not an island. He was not a maverick who did whatever He wanted. In John 8:28, Jesus said,

"When you lift up the Son of Man, then you will know that I am He, and I do nothing on My own initiative, but I speak these things as the Father taught Me."

Jesus lived in total dependence on God. He chose to live in dependence on the kindness of others, and He depended on the disciples to spread His message after He was gone. That's a lot of dependence. I realize I need to be increasingly more dependent on God, and what I'm now learning is that I need to be more dependent on the Christians around me too. If I allow my life to become intertwined with theirs…to let them know my weaknesses and failures, my struggles and hopes, and to understand theirs…I am following Jesus's example and He will be honored. As I do this, I grow. I am in constant dialogue with other Christian friends, that often disclose things that I would not come up with on my own. My soul is encouraged and refreshed in ways it would never be otherwise. Responding well to these kinds of blessing…the ones that hurt and the ones that refresh…are one part of what "victory in Christ" looks like. They only come from a concerted pursuit of dependence. But even though this idea is contradictory today because we hide behind our glass homes and picket fences as if we have it all together, we are lost, alone and hurting. To my own demise at times, pursuing this victory in Christ is more surprising and wonderful than I expected.

"Whatever your lips utter you must be sure to do, because you made your vow freely to the Lord your God with your own mouth" (Deuteronomy 23:23).

The polarity of controlling the flow of the tongue, is not fully understood until we experience the result of 'out of the abundance of the heart the mouth will speak". I am no longer amazed at what comes out of people, especially when what follows is "I really didn't mean it that way" I finally realized that when communicating we must be cognizant in terms of what we are saying and how we are saying it. If we communicate out of a dark place as the husband, she will be drawn to a dark place, which will create a gap in the continuous flow of your interaction. In a closed-loop system this is referred to as a "backlash." The resulting effect of backlash in a closed-loop system is tremendous pressure on the other recipient. In fact, instead of causing the other one to draw closer, that pressure drives them in the opposite direction. The result in a one-flesh relationship is the same. Anytime we place demands on each other to change, the resulting pressure creates just the opposite of what we wish to achieve. The only way to bring the power for change into our spouse's life is through intercessory prayer on each other's behalf. Keep it the standard to "Pray it on them; don't lay it on them." The pressure for change then comes from God Who also supplies the power for that change. Both the power and the pressure then flow from above and the dynamic flow between husband and wife remains stable. Furthermore, to maintain victory, we must be sensitive to the spirit of God, in the polarity of opposing differences as He directs us to move to a greater or lesser degree in any area. If that area is clearly scripturally assigned to one specific partner, then we automatically know who is to flow predominantly in that area. If one spouse is out of order in how he or she is flowing, it is not corrected by the other spouse flowing out of God's will. Additionally, in a crisis, all affected people take in information differently, process information differently, and act on information differently. As disciples we need to know that the way you normally communicate with your spouse and those around may not be effective during or after a crisis. Therefore, remember not to respond quickly, put the offended first, don't play the blame game and be transparent.

DESTINY

Some call me a child. Some say I'm wild.
Others say a teen that hasn't been weaned.
I drift from here to there and don't see the sign that read beware.
Tossing and turning within my sleep dreaming of someone to help me peak.
Sometimes up and sometimes down; I Just can't seem to find solid ground.
I reach out to touch someone's hand, but they are far away in a distant land.
All I need is someone near that will help me see life, and what its worth for you
And me.

Chapter 20

Emotionally & Intelligently Touched Intermittently

Research has taught us that newlywed couples are more apt to succeed and be transformed in the honeymoon stage. Men are  emotionally intelligent therefore research shows this type of husband honors and respects his wife, he will be open to learning more about emotions from her. He will come to understand her world and those of his children and friends. Unfortunately, most men, do not automatically shift. Let alone operate in the yielded husband's role. For centuries men were expected to oversee their families; with a sense of responsibility and entitlement, which got passed down from father to son, in so many subtle ways; that revising the husband's role can be a challenge for many men, even in these days when 60 percent of married women, work outside the home. The polarity of differences often drives both economic powers and self-esteem from their jobs. A significant number of the core issues we see between couples today have to do with this change in gender roles. Often, wives complain that men still aren't doing their fair share of domestic chores and childcare. This is not just an issue for young couples. We have observed the same pattern among partners in their forties and sixties. Men who are willing to accept influence are happily married. Those who are unwilling see their marriages become unstable. Perhaps the fundamental difference between husbands who accept influence and those who don't is that the former has learned that often in life you need to yield to win. When you drive through any busy city, you encounter frustrating bottlenecks and unexpected barricades that block your rightful passage. You can take one of two approaches to these impossible situations. One is to stop, become righteously indignant, and insist that the offending obstacle move. The other is to drive around it. The first approach will eventually earn you a heart attack. The second approach…which I call yielding to win…will get you home. The classic example of a husband yielding to win concerns the ubiquitous toilet seat issue. It's common for a woman to get irritated when her husband always leaves the toilet seat up, even though it only takes her a millisecond to put it down herself. For many women, a raised toilet seat is symbolic of the male's sense of entitlement. So, a man can score major points with his wife just by putting the seat down. The wise husband smiles at how smart he is as he drops the lid. The accepting influence is an attitude, but it's also a skill that you can home in on, if you pay attention to how you relate to your spouse. In your day-to-day life, this means working on the principles of following advice and exercise, of paying attention to your experience. Also…when you have a conflict, the key is to be willing to compromise. You do this by searching through your partner's request for something you can agree to. If despite plenty of effort as husband you are still unable to accept influence on an issue, it's a sign that an unacknowledged, unsolvable problem is stymieing his attempts. In such a case, the key is to learn how to cope with the gridlock, think about and reread your purpose to the wife as your role as husband. For example, love her the way Christ loved the Church (Ephesian 5). I submit, years of researching the scriptures year after year, for ways of understanding how, Jesus loves the church, inevitably calls me to echo his love for me in my love for my wife, came with resistance. Yes, resistance… The opposing difference of spirit and flesh. As a husband, God calls you to love your wife like Jesus loves her, so meditate on his deep, complex, and unparalleled love.

The Paradox of Love isn't Stubborn. Jesus won't ever leave his bride. He says to her, "Behold, I am with you always, to the end of the age" (Matthews 28:20). His love for your wife

128

is based not on her performance, but on his covenant love for her. When we keep our marriage covenants through all the challenges and changes over years of commitment, we reflect his kind of stubborn, delight-filled love. May our wives know the comfort of love that says, "I will never leave you nor forsake you" (Hebrews 13:5). Just as important is hope in love, when Jesus looks at your bride, he sees her as already sanctified. This hope is anchored in the power and promise of the gospel. Paul writes to believers, "You were washed, you were sanctified, you were justified in the name of the Lord Jesus Christ and by the Spirit of our God" (1Corthian 6:11). In fact, he sees her not only as already sanctified, but as already glorified (Roman 8:30). How often would your wife say that your love for her "hopes all things" (1Corhtinas 13:7)? By keeping eternity in mind, you can have patience with your wife, just as Jesus does with her and you. Even more important …is pursuing love, Jesus never takes a break from pursuing your wife's heart, not romantically but persistently. In fact, he cares not only about her devotion, but also her affection (Psalm 37:4). He is the tireless Shepherd who leaves the ninety-nine to seek after the one (Luke 15:4-7). In a similar way, God is glorified when a husband continually seeks a deeper relationship with his wife. A husband who has been captured by Jesus's love is an incurable romantic toward his wife. Along those line, having a forgiving love, Jesus gives your wife grace when she doesn't deserve it. It may be that the most Christlike thing you can do is offer your wife forgiveness daily, remembering that you too need forgiveness. The picture of forgiving love that every husband should seek, would be to emulate, Jesus making breakfast for Peter, who had sinned against him, denying him three times at his crucifixion (John 21:12-15). Is it you or your wife who is usually the first to begin to move toward reconciliation when it's needed? Likewise, joyful love is not just putting up with your wife or grudgingly but persistently loving her. He delights to be with his bride. He receives joy by giving us joy (Hebrew 12:2).

Wives who are loved this deeply, who know their husbands love to love them, are often an even greater blessing to others. Love your wife so joyfully that it's obvious to her and others. Jesus also served her in life and death. There is nothing that God can call you to do for your wife that would be too much! Jesus "gave himself up for her" (Ephesian 5:25). Many husbands think of themselves as kings to be served, but you and I are called by God to be the chief servants in our homes. The way to be like Christ in our marriages is through joining Jesus in taking up the towel and the basin (John 13:12-17).

The Sanctifying Love of Jesus reflects in how he loves your wife by helping her to grow in holiness and by being her advocate before the Father (1John 2:1). Do you encourage your wife to go to bible study, even if it means you must care for the kids by yourself for the evening? Do you regularly bring your wife before the father in prayer? Work hard to help your wife blossom spiritually. Likewise, Jesus leads us to what is good for us. Jesus not only loves your wife with a leading rather than a passive love, but he also leads her toward what is good (Psalms 23:2). It is impossible to lead our wives spiritually if we ourselves are not being led by God through the word and prayer. One way you can lead her well is by seeking her input and then making big decisions (and accepting the consequences), rather than allowing the decisions and consequences to fall to her. Jesus also provides your wife with all that she needs. Do you notice your wife's needs, even beyond physical provision, and do you make attempts to do something about it? Christ nourishes her, providing an environment for growth and flourishing. The apostle Paul explains to us that "in the same way husbands should love their wives as their own bodies" (Ephesian 5:28).

I must admit when I married my wife, it made a marked difference in our marriage, I realized that it was my responsibility to do what I could to fill my wife's sails.

Additionally, having the knowledge of loving her gave me the confidence to love her through Jesus. In conclusion, Jesus knows your wife better than she knows herself. He has an informed love for her. He knows her strengths, her weaknesses, and he acts on her behalf (Ephesian 5:29-30). While we will never know our wives like God knows them, he wants us to know them as well as we can. Our prayers for them will always be hindered if we fail to know them (1Peter 3:7). Our wives know they are cherished when we try to really know them. Husbands, we have an enemy, that ancient serpent, who desires to sift his way into our homes and cause havoc. But praise God if we know Jesus Christ. We will know He already defeated him. Know this, that when you love your wife like Jesus loves her, the foundation of your marriage is strengthened, Satan is defeated again, and Christ is lifted for the world to see.

THE STORM

Though the storm keeps on raging in my life, 'til sometimes it's hard to see even the stars at night. for inside my heart I just can't seem to fight,
Yet I know the fear that the night can bring is only a stepping-stone to all my dreams. So, now with this thought in mind, I'll lean on the maker 'til the end of time. Preparing my soul for his return. The storm, the time is only a twinkle of the universe,
And I am part of what was and is to be.

Chapter 21

Touched To Managing Conflict

The Paradox of conflict provides the framework with which to analyze conflict and to pinpoint the true issue being faced  to facilitate the implementation of the best possible solution. The polarity of opposing differences can be managed with the right attitude in conflict, thus finding specific techniques for handling marital troubles, whether perpetual or solvable. But first, you must recognize that negative emotions are important. Although it is stressful to listen to your partner's negative feelings, remember that successful relationships live by the motto. "When you are in pain, the world swoops in and listen." Conflict is everywhere, and conflict skills are valuable far beyond the spiritual realm.

It wasn't until God touched me that I began to understand the value of conflict and that without the trouble no matter how bad or good it seemed, there was a purpose for them all. You can never understand what it feels like to be up, without going down. We really must know who God is. He is the I' AM in everything that is and is to come. Therefore, all things are for His purpose alone. Pharaoh had an element of Good by letting the people go. He also had an element of bad by imprisoning them also. This is true even when your partner's anger, sadness, disappointment, or fear is directed at you. Negative emotions hold important information about how to love each other better. It takes a lot of understanding and proficiency in attunement to be able to really hear what your partner is saying when he or she is upset. One of the goals of this book is to guide partners toward expressing their negative emotions in ways that allow each of us to listen without feeling attacked so that the message gets through in a manner that encourages healing rather than more hurt. These sorts of discussions can be tough for both parties. It will help if you can both acknowledge this and remember to be gentle with each other. No one is right. There is no absolute reality in marital conflict, only two subjective ones. This is true whether the disagreement is solvable or perpetual. We must understand that "There is no immaculate perception." It will help you resolve your differences if you remember this basic truth.

The paradox of Acceptance is crucial. It is virtually impossible for people to heed advice unless they believe the other person understands, respects, and accepts them for who they are. When people feel criticized, disliked, or unappreciated, they are unable to change. Instead, they feel under siege, and they dig in. Therefore, the basis for coping effectively with relationship issues, whether solvable or perpetual, is to communicate basic acceptance of your partner's personality. Before you ask your spouse to change the way he or she drives, eats, vacuums, or makes love, you must: make sure your partner feels known and respected rather than criticized or demeaned. There's a big difference between "Sheesh, you're a lousy driver! Slow down before you kill us!" and "I know you enjoy driving fast, but I get nervous. Could you please slow down?" Maybe that second approach takes a bit longer. But that extra time is worth it since it is the only method that works! Adults could learn something in this regard from research into child development. Children thrive when we express understanding and relay the message that they are loved and accepted, "warts and all." When couples are not able to do this, sometimes the problem is that they are unable to forgive each other for past differences. It's all too easy to hold a grudge. For a marriage to go forward happily, you need to pardon each other and give up on past resentments. This can be hard to do, but it is well worth it. When you forgive your spouse, you both benefit. Bitterness is a heavy burden. As Shakespeare wrote in The Merchant of Venice, mercy is "twice blessed. It blesses him that gives and him that takes." Moreover, beliefs are the single most important aspect you can work on to get where you need to be in your life. If you want to know how important your beliefs are, you must imagine you're going underwater while holding your breath. Don't breathe for a minute, when you can't hold it any longer you realize how important air is for survival. Notwithstanding This is how important beliefs are in your life, every decision you make is generated by beliefs; the decisions you make shape your entire life. Therefore, your beliefs shape and improve your life, by one word. Faith. You reap what you are sowing verbally.

The polarity in whatever you are sowing is a form of what you believe in, whether it be negative or positive. All beliefs are formed naturally by living your life, through your own experience. What you observe, you learn. They form one with the other. Then, based on what you believe to be true equals your system of beliefs, but what happens when your truth is challenged? You look for anything (arguments, emotions, situations) that are right. This can generate conflicts or situations when you are suffering. This challenge can create a positive paradigm shift, or a negative downward spiral in your thinking and or beliefs. When you understand that what you believed isn't true, new beliefs are formed and you start believing differently, allowing your heart and mind to form a difference of opinion toward the unbelief. It is there you are well on your way of becoming the Covenant Partner that Christ has called you to. Now… No Other Way.

The polarity of differences within the construct of marriages is the responsibility of both husband and wife, however, the dependency on our partner and truth is our secure base. I'm not one to argue against certainty, for the scriptures were written and the creeds argued to establish theological and doctrinal certainties. To maintain the importance of paradox isn't the ambivalent shrug of postmodernity, which dismisses human capacity for objective knowledge. Instead, paradox gives a category for a different kind of certainty: "of truths that do not logically cohere." Instead of evading truth claims, paradox is a mechanism, affirming that truth, while knowable, can remain mysterious, beyond the reach of reason. While we are busy living as married couples, one of the most important areas of neglect is our communication. When we unearth the tension of paradox in the scriptures, we should move toward it with expectation, rather than from it in fear. To be left with tension, complexity, and mystery necessarily moves us toward humility; and knowing that he is God, and we are not. We long for something bigger and more enduring and more beautiful than our muddled, material lives. Thus, the reason I share this story...On the morning after an explosive argument with my wife, I came to the end of several conclusions with a clearer understanding of the way to move forward. Unsurprisingly, the conclusions were mostly built on both and the and. I needed to both persist in a ministry of loving words and a ministry of silent presence...because God had given me both the command to talk to my wife as a means of spiritual formation and the example of his own quiet ministry of kindness to Elijah, who'd arrived dejected and despairing on the other side of his confrontation with the prophets of Baal. As a both-and it was an answer full of tension and one that cast me back, not on my own understanding, but on God's. Unlike either and *or*, it was an answer that left me with the conviction that ongoing dependence on the Spirit's wisdom would be needed. The more we talk to each other, the more we will know about each other. This will help us respond to our spouse's needs, wants and desires. In our marriage, don't take your spouse for granted. Learn to ask important questions throughout every stage. Surprisingly... I suppose the sufficiency of the both-and is what Job discovered at the end of his long, angry tirade which God never saw fit to answer. "Who is this that darkens counsel by words without  knowledge? Dress for action like a man; I will question you, and you make it known to me. Where were you when I laid the foundation of the earth?" Job never got answers to his questions. He never had definitive reasons from God for why he had permitted his suffering. And the paradox is: *It was enough.* The polarity of our lives often leaves us confused, notwithstanding…In his letter to the Romans, the apostle Paul insisted on this paradox of being human, which is to say, in one sense, that we're both morally frail and morally aspiring. In Romans 7, he confesses his own tragic doubleness: "For I do not understand my own actions. For I do not do what I want, but I do the very thing I hate." In this, we're a mystery to ourselves: We fail the good that we will and indulge the evil that we hate. Empirically, I prove Paul's point every day. We're a mystery to ourselves: We fail the good that we will and indulge the evil that we hate; and as husbands, the paradox of being human is that we're both "chief of creatures" and "chief of sinners." Made in the image of God, we shared his moral likeness, loving the good and hating the evil in the very beginning. We were the "likeness of God walking in the garden," and our great grief, after the fall, was of a "broken man." Though we were meant to be like God and rule with him, we choose autonomy and rebellion over submission and worship. One bite of forbidden fruit destroyed us, self-loving creatures that we are paradoxically choosing to sin every time. In the garden, God graciously offered life, and we willingly refused it. Additionally, in the polarity of difference, we must remember the paradox of grace: the gospel announces both leniency and violence; mercy and judgment; rescue and death. What blazes up on Golgotha is God's embrace of contradiction: weakness as power, foolishness as wisdom. In conclusion, how could God allow his special creation, endowed with his likeness, to fall into disrepair? And if he did, could he call such apathy love? "It was impossible . . . that God should leave man to be carried off into corruption because it would be unfitting and unworthy of himself." It was God's glory, even his glory bequeathed to humanity, that demanded a rescue. The will of God was to redeem humanity by paradox: that falling short of the glory of God, he should be rescued to, once again, become like him. The reasons for salvation seem paradoxical; also consider the means. According to the great surprise of God's story, Jesus Christ didn't consider equality with God a thing to be grasped but made himself nothing, humbling himself to death on a cross. Remember...The firstborn of all creation became last, and humanity's life was found in God's own losing. Further, lest we think of Christ's self-sacrifice only as means to acquittal, we must remember the paradox of grace: the gospel announces both leniency and violence; mercy and judgment; rescue and death. What blazes up on Golgotha is God's embrace of contradiction: weakness as power, foolishness as wisdom.

It's a paradox to make men stumble to walk in righteousness. The command to all husband was to love her as Christ loved the church, therefore; Theology and Christian living are not oil and water; they are organically connected like seed and tree. If we are to live biblically in between the times, we must trust indicatives and obey imperatives."

Chapter 22

Touched Intermittently in my Anger

Anger is a signal that something is wrong and needs to be addressed. Sin and injustice are things we should be angry  about because we serve God that is just. It's important for us to understand that anger can be a gift if handled rightly. In my past I had to really face the noticeable anger that was in my life... the suppressed undealt with anger from self-inflicted pain of suicide, abandonment, the mental and the physical abuse. Arguably to better understand the anger, I had to understand how to be angry and not sin. Psychology defines anger as one of the basic human emotions, as elemental as happiness, sadness, anxiety, or disgust. These emotions are tied to basic survival and were honed over the course of human history. Anger is related to the "fight, flight, or freeze" response of the sympathetic nervous system; it prepares humans to fight. But fighting doesn't necessarily mean throwing punches. It might motivate communities to combat injustice by changing laws or enforcing new norms. Of course, anger too easily or frequently mobilized can undermine relationships or damage physical health in the long term. Prolonged release of the stress hormones that accompany anger can destroy neurons in areas of the brain associated with judgment and short-term memory and weaken the immune system. As a result, I struggled with chronic anger, and experienced occasional outbursts. I had to learn skills to identify and navigate this powerful emotion that would lead to growth and change in my life. For this reason, the question of why I shrugged off some annoyances while exploding in others, regardless anger results from a combination of the triggers and event, in my case it was the environment of my home, and the possible non-appraisal of parents. The trigger event that provokes anger, such as being cut off in traffic or yelled at by a parent.

The qualities of the individual include personality traits, such as narcissism, competitiveness, and low tolerance for frustration, and the pre-anger state, like levels of anxiety or exhaustion.

Perhaps most importantly is cognitive appraisal...appraising a situation as blameworthy, unjustified, punishable, etc. The combination of these components determines if, and why, people get mad. Nevertheless...what does it mean 'Be angry and sin not'? Anger is not a wrong emotion or feeling; we however need to determine what drives us to be angry and how we can manage it. We repeatedly express our resentment in sinful manners. "Be angry and do not sin; do not let the sun go down on your anger and give no opportunity to the devil. Example.... Let the thief no longer steal, but rather let him labor, doing honest work with his own hands, so that he may have something to share with anyone in need. Let no corrupting communication come out of your mouths, but only such as is good for building up, as fits the occasion, that it may give grace to those who hear." Ephesians 4:26-29 ESV. Paul speaks of living as a new person. Ephesians 4:17-32 is an important, exceptionally viable clarification of how to carry on with a Christian life. Paul takes note of the distinction between a day-to-day existence floundering under the force of transgression, instead of a day-to-day existence flourishing in the power of Christ.

I would like to suggest that as a Christians we are to approach life by setting aside or put away the things that trap unbelievers. This incorporates sins like perniciousness, criticism, upheaval, and harshness. All things being equal, we ought to exhibit a Christ-like disposition of adoration, love, pardoning, and forgiveness. To further emphasize…Paul's statement in verse 25 proceeds by handling the subject of outrage or anger. Two standards are given. To begin with, Paul instructs that anger itself is not a wrongdoing; there are a few things Christians should be irate about. God communicates anger (Exodus 4:14). Jesus showed controlled displeasure against the tax collectors when he turned over the tables (John 2:13-17). Be that as it may, uncontrolled displeasure and anger can lead to committing a transgression. Being irate is not a pardon to sin or an excuse to commit sin. Discretion is needed to direct anger in a God-regarding way. One approach to controlling outrage is given by Paul in his subsequent order, "Let not the sun go down upon your wrath" (Ephesians 4:26). The attention is not on the actual sunset, as though there is a certain time of day when all annoyances must be disregarded. The fact is we should not allow time to pass prior to managing any anger. Christians are to focus on managing their anger in a proper way and at a proper time. If not, harshness or the longing for retaliation can develop, prompting more wicked thinking and negative activities. As a result, anger can be a useful feeling if dealt with cautiously and rapidly to not prompt sin. It is anything but intended for us to continually live in anger, just that we managed our anger. The Bible does not reveal to us that we ought not to feel anger, however, it calls attention to handle our displeasure appropriately. Whenever ventilated negligently, anger can hurt others and obliterate our relationships and may just result in unfavorable circumstances.

Historically…anger un-restrained can become severe and destroy us from the inside. Paul even advises us to manage our resentment promptly in such a way that develops our relationships instead of tearing them down. On the off chance that we nurture our displeasure, we will offer Satan a chance to separate us. If we are irate and angry with somebody at this moment, how would we be able to deal with or resolve our disparities? Try not to allow the day to end before we start to deal with retouching our relationships.

Today is the best day of the rest of your life.

BLUES AND GRAYS

Sculptured clays, puzzles, and maze.
Burning candle lights, on a starlit night.
The chasing of rainbows while walking in
The rain.
Reminiscing all the joy and the pains,
Crisp brooks, shallow streams, and water
falls. In the distance, mountains arrayed in thunder.
Soft clouds feel the skies, rainbows arrayed with violets and
rose colors.
Blues and grays nestled in the skies heat still forms wonders
for our eyes, Glittering eyes, and soft cheeks.
A gentle touch from His embrace is all it takes.

Chapter 23

The Polarity of the Chest less Man

Paul declares that Christians are "under grace" (Romans 6:14). That means we are no longer enslaved to sin  (indicative; (Romans 6:6). But that also means we don't let sin reign in our mortal bodies (imperative; (Romans 6:12). How do we do that? We let indicatives fuel our obedience to God. Recall what is already true to be obedient in the not yet. Suppose, for example, that you're feeling spiritually lethargic. After seeing or thinking about something tempting, you sense sin in your heart being aroused in your mortal body, and you long to satisfy its demands. Sin's objective is to satisfy you with cheap thrills and empty offers of satisfaction. And now, you think that sounds like a great idea; during those moments, they are not... remind yourself of what is true of you in Christ. Pray God's word over your sin-stricken soul. Say, "The same Spirit that raised Jesus from the dead, that spiritually raised me from the dead in him, dwells in me powerfully (Romans 8:11; Ephesians 1:19–20)! Think about that reality for a second. You have divine power at your disposal. You have access to a storehouse of strength for the battle. God doesn't leave you to fend for yourself. He equips you for the fight (Philippians 2:12–13). The Spirit that raised our Lord from death enables us to "put to death the deeds of the body" (Romans 8:13). And so, we fight. Putting it all together, I finally began understanding the power of Christs statement. "He that is great among you should be your servant." A man is not defined by how far your chest sticks out. Your emotional Intelligence refers to your ability to recognize and manage your own emotions, recognize, and respond to the emotions of others and always build effective relationships. Developing self-awareness promotes increased fruitfulness and higher contentment. These changes can also lead to improved communication, increased empathy, and better interpersonal rapport and relationships. Think about that reality for a second. You have divine power at your disposal. You have access to a storehouse of strength for the battle. God doesn't leave you to fend for yourself. He equips you for the fight (Philippians 2:12–13). The Spirit that raised our Lord from death enables us to "put to death the deeds of the body" (Romans 8:13). And so, we fight. We don't claim perfect victory, but we also don't claim utter defeat. In between the times, we rest on what is true of us in Christ, and we fight until that day when faith become sight, and everything in the not yet becomes ours.

The Chest less Man Paradox of love

The polarity of differences in the paradox of love in current society arises from a combination of the following two seemingly opposing claims…a greater percentage of intimate relationships are based on love; and a greater percentage of intimate relationships involve romantic compromises. Since romantic compromises are considered to run counter to love, how can these two claims co-exist? At its core, love is a fruit of the Holy Spirit (Galatians 5:22). As we walk in the Spirit, having "crucified the flesh with its passions and desires" (Galatians 5:24-25), we learn to put aside the deeds of the flesh (anger, pride, self-centeredness, and ungodliness) and put on the new self which is being renewed to a true knowledge according to the image of Jesus (Colossians 3). The new life is marked by humility, godliness, faithfulness, and putting the interests of others ahead of our own interests. That's the key to practical biblical love – sanctification by the Holy Spirit. Paul's list is simply a practical description of the contrast between the old life (unsanctified, carnal, or unsaved) and the new life (sanctified, transformed) we have in Christ.

143

Accordingly…Ephesians 3:15-16 "But speaking the truth in love, we are to grow up in all aspects into Him who is the head, even Christ, from whom the whole body, being fitted and held together by what every joint supplies, according to the proper working of each individual part, causes the growth of the body for the building up of itself in love." Be not deceived Look up the word "love" in any secular dictionary and you'll most likely find the definitions focus on words like attraction, affection, or feeling. These words are ambiguous and indefinable. At best, this kind of love may last for a few years. Attraction is frequently based on superficial traits; affection quickly fades when it's not reciprocated, and feelings are the most uncertain and changeable human trait of all!

The Paradigm shift of Love…. Is loving with intention and transparency, that requires a paradigm shift in how 'love' is defined. When we view love through God's divine lens it produces deeper relationships with others. The love paradigm shift challenges whether we can handle the tension of trusting God, to soothe us as we interact with difficult people. Think of a paradigm shift like this…Before you build a house, you need a blueprint for it – a pattern or plan for how the house will turn out. Paradigms are like blueprints, or plans, for specific results in your life. If you want to change something about the house you're building, you change the blueprints first. The same goes for shifting your paradigms to generate different results and understanding the polarity of differences in your life! This means that creating a paradigm shift is simply an awareness issue. Once you recognize that you have a paradigm in place, you have the power to change it. You have paradigms in place in all areas of your life… maybe without even knowing it; creating major results in your life i.e., time, money, freedom, wellbeing, relationships, and vocation – and chances are you already have firm paradigms in place in each area, some of which may be limiting you towards your purpose.

Your marriage Paradigms shifts aren't inherently good or bad.

They're either expansive – serving you and creating growth in an area of your life, or contractive – creating subconscious blocks and challenges. Some of your paradigms are likely working great for you, while others may be keeping you stuck. And if you want to know what your paradigms are producing in your life, all you must do is look at your current results – because your results are a mature mirror for the paradigms that you think from and live by. If you have a dream for your life but that dream is not happening for you, the great news is that you can change your paradigms to better service and manifest your dream. This is called a paradigm shift, and all it requires is shifting your perspective. Throughout the course of your life, maybe you've heard the saying that you are a child of God. But what does that mean exactly? I believe it means that we didn't create ourselves. Not one of us has the higher intelligence to create our own bodies or organize our brains into the magnificent interfaces they are – complex systems that can communicate with both the finite and infinite sides of our nature.

That's why…I believe we didn't create ourselves, we are the offspring of a deathless spirit, of an infinite intelligence, we can access this mind of infinite intelligence, and the amazing part of it all is; when we relate to our circumstances or conditions as spiritual beings having a human experience, we can tap into everything that the universe has to offer us! We were called into being to make a difference and to do extraordinary things. We were built to live a life of joy, fulfillment, abundance in Christ, and know your highest self.

Chapter 24

Intermittently Becoming a Man

Conversely...How has being a man changed? That's a tough question. On the one hand, the definition of  masculinity has expanded to include traditionally feminine virtues such as being nurturing and a hands-on parent. But until recently, the meaning of manhood had yet to come under scrutiny. And rightfully so! Consider the following facts that men are in the news for all the wrong reasons: mental illness, campus sexual assault, terrorism, mass shootings, and violence against woman. If we can discern what this type of behavior has done to our homes and community, can start the process of identifying how God you as a man. In contrast masculinity has eroded over the past 4 decades, with men redefining their gender to their own demise.

The polarity of manhood

I think there's good news and bad news, and it depends a lot on [context]: race, age, sexuality, region. It's a hard question to answer. The more you subscribe to traditional ideas of masculinity, the harder it may be today to construct a healthy idea of masculinity or to navigate this current world. My father's world was like *Father knows best;* everybody knew their place. The men smoked in elevators and drank hard liquor during the weekday. They ruled their home with an iron fist, beat their woman into submission and like much of our society today we reenact this on television and within sport...as if the abuse is normal, obviously due to making someone money. Consequently, I grew up thinking that my world would look like that. The reality, however, is many of our sons have these expectations, and we know this, and we are fine with that. Young men don't see enough of what it really means to be a nurturing, caring, great man of Christ. As a result, there are males and there are men. Men are easy to spot. They're strong and tough and dangerous. They're the guys you call when you need help. They're dependable, self-reliant. They're creating something, a place in this world, in leadership role as a servant. We need more of them. Hopefully, I can shed some light that will help you better understand what it means to be a man by better defining the characteristics that make up this ideal. Generally, we define men in the following vernacular, toughness, persisting through the pain. Men do not succumb to pain. We do not allow it to stand in the way of the goal, or simply what must be done. We are stoic... a man does not worry about the opinions of others. He concerns himself only with what he can control. He's not a worrier, he's a warrior; depending on Christ and not himself. Depending on Christ is learned over time. If you're not quite there, remember to stay on the path, it's a journey that never ends. Furthermore... your manliness demands that you're not only a good man morally, but that you're good at being a man from a utility standpoint, and men are men so they can protect and defend. If you have no capacity for danger, you're not doing this masculinity thing very well. To embrace the concept of a *chest less man* and becoming successful is as necessary for our souls as air for our ability to live another day. You represent to the world your loyalty to Christ in how you carry yourself, how you act, the work you get completed, is a witness to someone. In addition. You cannot be a man and be completely refined and polished and well-mannered. You must be rough around the edges. You must be a little barbaric, a tad dangerous, a Viking at heart. Being a man means you're not fully civilized. There will always be an aspect of you that has the capacity to do harm, especially if it's for good. This would be a glimpse into some of the traits the world has defined as being man. Obviously…from the perspective of scripture, this is not what makes a man although welcoming, they do not give a real picture into the real definition of being a man. I recently discovered and investigated, "The 7 Men" by Eric Metaxas and the secret of their greatness. It is an examination of seven different men, with specific emphasis upon their unique contribution to the world because of their faith in Christ. The seven men highlighted are George Washington, William Wilberforce, Eric Liddell, Dietrich Bonhoeffer, Jackie Robinson, Pope John Paul II, and Charles Colson. In addition to chapters on each of these, there is an interesting introduction in which Metaxas argues that the idea of manhood is really in his sights. He writes that he wants the book to not talk about manhood, but instead be one that, "shows it in the actual lives of great men" In addition to chapters on each of these. These captivating stories of some of the most inspiring men in history. A gallery of greatness comes to life as Metaxas reveals men who faced insurmountable struggles and challenges with victorious resolve. The book has some great points; however, I felt it missed the true reflective marks of being a man. Based on my finding's scripture reflect that Jesus Christ is a true human being, clear from the verses below that he was indeed a man. Acts 2:22. "Men of Israel, listen to this: Jesus of Nazareth was a man accredited by God to you by miracles, wonders, and signs, which God did among you through him, as you yourselves know. Acts 2:23. At some point or another, every man questions his personal virility. "Am I, a real man?" "Am I man enough?" Most of us have our own opinion about what it means to be a real man. Strong! Courageous! A great leader! Characteristics like these come to mind when we think of the ideal man. Personally, when I think of the epitome of someone who conquered manhood I think of Jesus, the *quintessence of strength, courage, love, and leadership.* With regards to Christ, I have found that the best way to attain success is to find someone who is living the attributes you are trying to achieve and then emulate them. Knowing that Jesus is considered the epitome of manhood, in life we should all strive to be like HIM. The truth is to possess a fraction of the characteristics of Jesus would be to achieve our greatest triumph.

Unconventionally our pursuit of excellence will adhere and emulate and master the touch of being compassionate. When  He saw the crowds, he had compassion on them because they were bewildered and helpless, like sheep without a shepherd. (Matthews 9:36). Jesus never avoided helping people. In fact, he always looked upon them and offered compassion. For some, it was physical healing while for others spiritual fostering was needed. In any case, Jesus always took the time to notice the hurting individual and His compassion drove Him to help them. To be a mature man we need to open our eyes at the opportunities to show compassion. In a self-involved world, all it takes is us slowing down and recognizing the underline pain in others. The chest less man seeks to be a servant. The Son of Man did not come to be served but to serve, and to give his life as a ransom for many. (Mark 10:45). Jesus was the ultimate servant. Despite having the authority to rein over everything, He displayed the exact opposite by lowering himself and serving others. Humility at its highest, after washing His disciples' feet, He said, "An example I have given you, that you should do likewise." (John 13:15). The chest less man understands that success comes as a derivative of serving others. Success and happiness are unintended side effects of one's personal dedication to a cause greater than oneself or as the by-product of one's surrendering to serve others. The chest less man is loving. Greater love has no man than this, that a man lay down his life for his friends. (John 15:13). Jesus' love was evident through his compassion and serving deeds. His greatest manifestation of love, however, was His self-sacrifice while on the cross bearing our sins so that we may live. Jesus instructed that the way we love in fact is an indicator that we are His disciples (John 13:35). Arguably Jesus instructs us on how to be mature men, and therefore how to love our spouse (Ephesians 5:28-33), and how to love our neighbor (Mark 12:31). These three remain: faith, hope, and love. But the greatest of these is love. (1 Corinthians 13) A mature man is a loving man.

In contrast to our culture, revenge is the first thing we seek when wronged. A mature man seeks to be forgiving. Jesus said, "Father, forgive them, for they don't know what they are doing." (Luke 23:35). Among all His miracles, I find this act of forgiveness to be the most amazing. Even during all His pain, in a situation where any other man would be thinking an eye for an eye. Jesus had the ability to forgive those causing Him pain in the very act of His anguish. To be a mature man we must forgive, if we are unable to forgive then we do not love. If we do not love, then we are not His disciples.

The chest less man has *integrity*. Jesus turned and said to Peter, "Get behind me, Satan! You are a stumbling block to me; you do not have in mind the concerns of God, but merely human concerns." (Matthew16:23). Integrity to call it as it is — Jesus was bold and undivided, cohesive in his truthfulness. Being boldly honest is difficult to do especially towards those closest to us. Yet in Jesus, we see straight truthfulness towards every person He dealt with: His disciples, the religious leaders, those who came in brief contact with Him. This means that a mature man's integrity is above reproach; we need to have no fear in telling the truth. Be a man of integrity; let your yes be yes and your no be no. (Matthew 5:37). Further evidence proves the chest less man expresses gentleness. "Let the little children come to me, and do not hinder them." (Matthew 19:14). There were times when Jesus used stern words, but He knew when gentleness was appropriate. Children seemed to love coming to him, and He made sure the disciples knew not to hinder them when they did so. His tenderheartedness and kindness were evident when speaking to His Disciples, mother, or other ladies. But, when He was giving someone a rebuke or making a point in a tutoring, He knew when turning up the heat was necessary and only did so strategically. He went a little further and said, "My Father, if it is possible, may this cup be taken from me. Yet not as I will, but as you will." (Matthew 26:39). Jesus had no lack of commitment whatsoever. Wherever He was, or whomever He was with, He was fully in the moment and committed to His goals. Even to the point of physical torture, He knew it was the only way to pay for everyone's sins (His goal), so He stayed committed even when his mission deemed unbearable. The chest less man has *deep convictions* to his commitments, like Jesus we must have laser focus on our goals so we can stay on track and finished strong. That is why. A chest less man must have *patience*. Whoever is patient having great understanding, but one who is quick-tempered displays folly. (Proverbs 14:29). Throughout the gospels, Jesus clearly gets portrayed as a very patient man. He was surrounded by disciples who constantly doubted Him, Pharisees who continually attacked Him, and large crowds who wouldn't leave Him alone. Despite it all, He kept His composure and responded appropriately to every individual.

A mature man is patient like a farmer who waits for the precious fruit of the earth, and has patience for it, until he receives the early and latter rain. (James 5:7). For this reason, a mature man needs *self-control*. Christ our High Priest knows and understands our weaknesses, for he faced all the same testing we do, yet he did not sin. (Hebrews 4:15). Jesus was human, he was tempted in every way just like you and me. He spent time being tempted by the devil in the wilderness, who offered Him food, power, and many other things. Jesus controlled His desires and submitted them all to the will of the Father. Yes, He had desires for food and other things, but He had a greater desire to obey the Lord and accomplish what He set out to do. The chest less man is *self-controlled* and has the discipline to take every thought captive and make it obedient to stay on track and finish strong. (2 Corinthians 10:5). In conclusion a mature man strives for maturing in Christ. Therefore, you are to be mature, as your heavenly Father is mature. (Matthew 5:48). A man may never attain maturation, but with the continual chase he might obtain excellence. Albert Einstein was quoted saying, "A maturing of means, and confusion of aims, seems to be our main problem." A mature man understands that his aim is to emulate Jesus, understanding his characteristics and habitually following them is the shortest path to maturation.

The world doesn't need more role models; it needs more men with the characteristics of Christ of Jesus on display.

SLEEP MY CHILD

It is a glorious winter morning.
As I face this New Year through,
May I identify with your resolutions
past and present of the things
You want me to do.
Then, as the sun begins to set and darkness
walks quietly in; let the night be to me a
Comforting blanket that scans to no end.
It can no longer bring its fears; but rather,
Has become a glorious finale. Now as I lie down to sleep,
remind me that you are just a prayerful whisper away.
Sleep my Child!

Chapter 25

Intermittent language of love

The Ultimate example of Love displayed. I must admit. What the heck is that? Namely we refer to it as acts of service. Quality...time...Words....   of....

Affirmation...Physical touch...Communication...Expressions of Affection and Love...Final thought. In the polarity of differences, we can construct the basis for affirming love. In contrast, how does Christ show love? Historically Isaiah 49:16 says God loves you so much that He engraved your name on the palm of His hand. Matthew 10:30 says He loves you so much that He knows how many hairs are on your head. Psalms 56:8 says He loves you so much that He saves your tears in a bottle. Jeremiah 31:3 says He loves you with everlasting love. God's love is very personal toward you. It doesn't matter where you've been, it doesn't matter what you've done, it doesn't matter what you've experienced - God loves you. It doesn't matter what you have thought about yourself or what other people may have said about you - God loves you. This is what God says about you! You are honored, you are precious in His eyes (Isaiah 43:4). Isn't that an amazing thing? Most often when the Bible attempts to express God's love, it makes a beeline for the cross of Jesus Christ. The cross is God's statement of just how much He loves you. When you think of the immensity of God's love, the first thing the Bible often asks us to do is to consider the price that was paid. This is love: not that we loved God, but that He loved us and sent His Son as an atoning sacrifice for our sins. (1 John 4:10). Until now. What makes this love so amazing is that it is highlighted against the backdrop of a debt that each one of us owes. At the core of God's being is His holiness. For us to have any kind of relationship with Him, we must find a way for our sins to be forgiven. However, the problem is, there's nothing we can do to accomplish that - it's too big of a debt. We can't buy God's favor, we can't work for it, we can't ever be good enough to earn it. God's holiness demanded that sin be paid for, and then God's love found a way. I proclaim this great love to you today. God loves you with an everlasting love that words fail to describe.

The word love we use all the time, right? Sometimes we hear the expression of love in, "I love pizza, my wife, and my dog," and you're hoping they don't mean that in all the same way, but what this leads to us realizing is that this word that we use a lot, does not take on the full meaning of expression oftentimes. In my experience, I'm not sure people know what they are saying let alone the meaning. Consequentially this reminds me of that scene from the movie "The Princess Bride" where Inigo Montoya says, "You keep using that word. I do not think it means what you think it means." Sometimes someone will say that one action is loving, and someone will say the exact opposite of that action is loving, so what we must determine as Christians who have the Bible as our authority is, what is love? Is it simply support? Is it encouraging? Is it giving someone what they want? Is there even a right answer to this question? That would be an important question to answer. Is love just the type of thing where I look inwardly and determine what I think it is, what I like, or what feels best, or is there another option? Perhaps more pertinent for cultural situation today, can an action be loving if the person receiving the action doesn't think it's loving? Is it loving to tell someone they're wrong? Is there a right or wrong way to do that, or is that always wrong? These are the types of questions that we're confronted with as Christians living in America today, so I have two modest goals today. The first is to look at the theological: What is love? What is a biblically based, God-grounded definition of love? The second is the practical: How can we apply that biblically based definition that we come up with to our everyday life, to situations we often find ourselves in? We can't look inward to arrive at this answer. However, we must realize it's not good or bad...its good and bad. If everyone were to look inward and say, "What do I think love is, and that's the actual right answer," there could be as many right answers as there are people here today, so what we must first acknowledge is there is a right and a wrong answer. Now we may disagree about what that is, but we at least must establish that there is a right answer to this question. In addition, when we're looking for right answers to hard questions we need to go to Scripture, so our passage for today, among many, is going to be Romans 5, and this is where we see Paul, writing under the inspiration of the Holy Spirit saying..." When we were utterly helpless, Christ came at just the right time and died for us sinners. Now, most people would not be willing to die for an upright person, though someone might perhaps be willing to die for a person who is especially good, but God showed his great love for us by sending Christ to die for us while we were still sinners. Since we have now been justified by his blood, how much more will we be saved from God's wrath through him?" Additionally... This passage links God's ultimate love, by sending Christ to die on the cross, so when we want to understand love, a good starting point option would be to fix our sight on the cross. Generally speaking. John 3:16 says," For this is the way God loved the world." You want to know how God loved the world? Look here. Well, he gave me his one and only son. That's how he loved the world. He committed him to the cross. In addition... Paul, writing in Galatians 2, says, "I have been crucified with Christ and it's no longer I who live but Christ who lives in me, and the life which I now live in the flesh I live by faith in the son of God, who loved me and gave himself up for me." How did he love me? He gave himself up on the cross, furthermore, in Ephesians, we see, "Walk in love, just as Christ also loved you and gave himself up for you," and a few verses later Paul links this loving example interestingly enough; that Christ sacrificially gave on the cross to show husbands how to love their wives. Undoubtedly...we're starting to see the interment touch of love by way of the cross. Now, I don't think that should surprise us, but when we think about love, is the cross the first thing we think about?

Love is Intermittently understood through the Cross.

In 1 John, we see, "We know love by this, that he laid down his life for us," obviously the major point, which can only be

ascertained in love and best understood through the cross. The cross and the resurrection are the center point of history. Now, you may not think that, but everything in scripture before the crucifixion, was us to the redemption of man. Therefore, everything after the cross is to be considered the events worked out beforehand of the intent and purpose that God had planned from eternity past, so when we want to understand love, let's look at the cross and observe the attributes of the cross that we can distill and apply to our situation today. Historically...The cross was certainly the most visible act of God's love towards us. We can see this throughout his examples. Jesus Christ was an ordinary man on earth; with an extraordinary since of responsibility; he was focused from childhood of the plan that was carved in his heart. Consequentially that decision was made long before the world was created and this act of love makes it impossible to comprehend this gift of love and devotion, as his spirit is poured out to the faithful, purifying them, offering them heavenly strength, rousing them to the attainment of all virtues, recalling those wise words of the Apostle St. James, "Every gift and every perfect gift is from above, coming down from the Father of Lights...It may be that... We think of the

cross as being about us. In contrast the cross is about God primarily and we are beneficiaries of the work that was done there. And the cross, first and foremost, was God glorifying himself in the creation of a people for himself, doing something only he could do. So, when we want to understand love, remember; it was planned out before the foundation of the world in God, for a people that had lost their way. His love was for us!

The cross is the way in which God shows his love for us, so love has a God-facing component, it often has a man and woman; facing component imbedded sacrificial, undeserved, and costly. Undoubtedly... it was an objective good. God said the cross therefore accomplished his plan, and we can briefly look at the cross and see that love is about man, its sacrifice. Still, there's a lot of confusion about love in our culture, surrounding and understanding the cross. Arguably some people will never understand exactly what happened at calvary. The significance of Jesus's profound love for us is demonstrated through His willingness to sacrifice His life for our sake. The love from His heart motivated all His actions; His inner life manifested in His demonstrated virtues and sacrifice. Yet this great love is often received with ingratitude, even by the faithful. The purpose of devotion to the Sacred Heart of Jesus is to focus our hearts on receiving and returning His love with gratitude, with all our heart, soul, and strength that He may be glorified. As Revelation 1:5-6 says, from Jesus Christ, the faithful witness, the firstborn of the dead and ruler of the kings of the earth. To him who loves us and has freed us from our sins by his blood, who has made us into a kingdom, priests for his God and Father, to him be glory and power forever [and ever]. Amen. As a result, we need to value not just what Jesus did at the cross, but what God showed at the cross. We have been let in on the greatest display of love and what it looks like. In short, we are to strive more earnestly and act accordingly towards all people, with a greater responsibility in how we love. We've looked at some attributes of the cross, and what I think would be helpful is to look at a definition. When we think of love, yes, let's think of the cross, but let's use a definition like this.

"Love is God-honoring action taken in response to God's grace for God's glory and/or a man's good,"

I think these captures what scripture underscores and defends against some of the errors in thinking about love today. This fits very well with what Christ did at the cross because what he did at the cross was for God's (his) glory. It was also for the good of mankind. All in all. This fits well for areas of life like parenting. Now as a parent in a parenting situation, oftentimes a parent will have the occasion to discipline a child, and let's just stipulate that there are two ways you could do this. You could do this out of anger and frustration, or you could take it out of love to train your child up to respect authority, to be more disciplined, to understand what a God-man authority structure looks like in the polarity of differences; the same action with two different intents, one can be without loving and the other, loving, our intent matters. Subsequently. How we parents treat our siblings, our parents, can display love, and the action itself can only be determined by the intent. Similarly giving is a clearer example when we gave the offering: Giving can be an act of love to God. However, if two people put $100 on the offering plate, we can't know which one of those was loving or not. If one person is doing it out of some type of obligation where they feel like they're "paying" their tithe and the other is doing it in response to the grace they've been shown, well the second one is certainly more loving than the first. Again, we often think about giving as something we do to God, in essence it is, for our good and it trains us to not hold onto things; it is a response to God's grace that's… for God's glory and for our good.

In contrast, the biblical definition is much deeper. Comparing the two is startling, like hanging a paint-by-number by a three-year-old next to Leonardo da Vinci's Mona Lisa or Michelangelo's Sistine Chapel. Scripture speaks much  about love. In the Bible, love is practical and tangible. It's made up of actions and words inspired by the will rather than some vague feeling that comes and goes on a whim. The most common word translated "love" is agape, which means affection and goodwill, with the motivation of benevolence. In other words, love does what is best for the one loved. It activates the will to respond in ways that benefit the object of our love. God is the original (and only) source of this kind of love. Furthermore Evangelism, gives a clearer example of God-centered love. We are responding to the grace, by doing it for the glory of God, and sharing something that is for man's good. A passage in Matthew says we should;" Love the Lord your God with all your heart, with all your soul, and with all your mind. This is the first and greatest commandment, and the second is like it. Love your neighbor as yourself," so, we see that there is a God-facing component to what we're told to do in love, and there is a "loving our neighbor" component. Oftentimes loving God sounds a little abstract. To illustrate, John 14 says, "If you love me, you will keep my commands," so we see that loving God is at least keeping his commands. It's not legalism by any means; but it does involve doing the things he's told us to do. Therefore, an action can't be loving, by definition, if it does not follow what God has laid out. He also says this a little later in John 14: "The person who has my commands and obeys them is the one who loves me. The one who loves me will be loved by my father, and I will love him," so what we see is that loving God fulfills this command, by loving other people. The clarifying statement of John 13, "Everyone will know by this… that you are my disciples, if you have love for one another.". Let's pause for a moment and be honest with ourselves; we aren't doing so well in loving our neighbor. If we're supposed to show the world that we are disciples by our love for one another. Our treatment of each other should be like a beacon that draws the attention of the world. For example…when we get hurt; we are quick to forgive, and welcome back into fellowship, that looks weird to the world, but smells good in the nostril of God. As a result, … I had to really learn how to forgive in love and let go of people that inadvertently hurt me. To forgive so that I could be forgiven and help this person to forgive themselves. Which ultimately helps the family, and the body of Christ. Similarly…Peter is asking Jesus how many times he should forgive a brother in Christ. Getting in Peter's mind, when he says, "Should it be seven?" he probably thinks he's shooting high, like, not three. "I'm going to forgive seven times. How's that, Jesus?" Jesus says, "How about 70 times seven?" and he's not saying, "Peter, you need to get a longer scroll so you can keep track of this." What he's saying is, there's no limit. The polarity of forgiving wasn't something I could just embrace. It was intermittently happening as I began to understand and accept the sovereignty of Christ in me. I had to be welcomed back into fellowship and be forgiven. The posture to repentance, and love will cause us to forgive, thus covering a multitude of sins. Hence. If the cross is the best example of God's great love and how to love, then love is the catalyst to life in Christ. Again…How can Jesus say that our love for each other will announce to others that we're his disciples? Because Christian love is different. It's not the "I love pizza" sort of love. It's a love of the cross, and no one can fully understand love without understanding the cross, so when we live in such a way and we love in such a way that draws the attention of the world and they say, "This is weird," why is it weird? Because they don't understand the cross. Because they don't understand the motivation for our love. They don't understand that we're responding to the grace of God that's been poured out in such a magnificent, powerful way. So, love is best understood through the cross. That's the theological point. When we want to understand love, we look at the cross. Love is a God-centered action taken in response to God's grace for God's glory and man's good, and I've had to repeat that many times because it's kind of a tongue twister, but it's important. It really captures what the Bible teaches on love. This means that we all need to study to show yourself approved unto God a workman, who is not ashamed but rightfully dividing the word of truth.

WHY HAVE WE FORGOTTEN

My people have forgotten me, days without number,
Long ago they closed their eyes and fell into a slumber. What can I do to wake them up from this deep sleep to get them to obey me and my laws and statues keep?
O turn backsliding children! For I am married unto you; and though you have forsaken me, to you I have been True.
Could a maid forget her ornament or a bride her attire? Yet, you have forgotten me; and me you've lost desire. Although in my forgiveness, I did wash your sins of scarlet, again you turn to strangers and begin to play the harlot.
Yet, my love still reaches out and follows where you go. I'll once again forgive and wash you white as snow. I can restore the joy and peace, removing all the blame.
For on the cross of Calvary, I took all the sin and shame.
Return backsliding man and feel the thunder of what was and is to be. I am door to all you are and to heaven; but you must Turn the key.

Chapter 26

Intermittent decisions of love

In a now famous commencement speech, actor Jim Carrey said that many of us often make decisions out of fear disguised  as practicality. Now being practical can be good, but the thing is, good is the enemy of great. The polarity of decisions made from a place of fear puts you in a contractive mindset, a mindset for dreaming small and accepting your current circumstances. If you feel you're making decisions based on fear, try shifting your perspective and making them based on love and not love or fear and you'll immediately begin to live more expansively. Instead of asking yourself what you think you should do, or what you might be capable of, ask yourself the resounding and powerful question...What would I LOVE? This one question will make you dream like a kid again. How do you begin to start reconnecting to what truly being loved and truly loving; versus looking at current circumstances, that display what you can be, do and have in your life? Consider. The vulnerability of love; is a necessary part of loving an individual. For you to love someone, you'll need to pull down your walls and allow this person in. You need to show him or her the person only you know yourself to be. What this does is make us transparent, and vulnerable to judgment, ridicule, that possibility might you scare you away. We can see this in a husband and wife, experiencing two strong competing emotions that seem to be at the crux of the dilemma of vulnerability, love, and pain. Although discomfort may be part of the equation, vulnerability stems from love, joy, and belonging, all of which are fundamental parts of the human experience. Moreover, research suggests that satisfying, intimate relationships are what gives our lives happiness, meaning, and purpose. Consequentially social isolation puts us at risk for psychological and physical issues such as depression and cardiovascular disease and increases our risk of mortality. That is why we are all worthy of emotional connection, but it starts with being authentic. To connect with your husband or wife, it is necessary to let go of who you think you should be or who you think your partner wants you to be; to make room for who you are. This means for connection to happen; we must allow our true selves to be seen and known and accept some discomfort. This becomes evident in our first step towards achieving our oneness; and realizing that you cannot control the unknown and the potential to be hurt, criticized, or rejected is part of the growth. Love is inherently uncertain and risky, and fear will only create distance and prevent you from being able to fully connect with your partner. Nevertheless…Allowing your partner to see your true self is not only important at the beginning of a relationship but is also necessary to maintain closeness for the relationship to lasts. In fact, according to the Divorce Mediation Project, 80% of divorced men and women reported that their marriage dissolved due to feelings of growing apart and a decreased sense of closeness. Furthermore, partners who reported distance in their relationship were more likely to behave in ways that were considered hostile. Along these lines relationships go through ebbs and flows wherein both partners experience changes in aspirations, values, interests, fears, and stressors. However, being vulnerable to sharing these feelings with your partner is essential for a healthy relationship. Ask yourself: "If you don't know someone, how can you truly love them?" The paradox of vulnerability is beneficial in the romantic relationships of male and female because it; allows us to build intimacy and connection, increases self-worth and builds our confidence. In addition, it promotes belongingness and acceptance, allowing us to build our trust in others, which enables us to give and receive love.

In conclusion, my wife, licensed psychotherapist Tasha Gooden encourages us to ask ourselves several tough questions regarding what's fueling our invulnerability. For instance, are you afraid of exposing parts of your personality that your partner may not like? Does keeping a distance make you feel safe and in control of your emotions? Do feelings of rejection or judgement stop you from sharing your true feelings or bringing up difficult topics? More specifically, do you feel that your partner will leave or betray you and view relationships as uninteresting or unimportant? Consequentially, this does not only apply to romantic relationships, but relationships in general. Whether you are interacting with a partner, family member, friend, or others; give them a glimpse into what makes you. Allow people to connect with your emotions and experiences. Maybe they will share their own story about a time where they also struggled and felt inadequate or lonely. Lastly, give yourself the opportunity to experience love and to be seen. And always remember, "you got to risk it to get the biscuit" – you must take risks to get rewards.

Chapter 27

Intermittent Appreciation

The ultimate expression of the law of polarity in relationships is sexual attraction and fulfillment and having a  balanced relationship within polarity to having intimate relationship that is sustainable. Yet... until you truly embrace and appreciate your partner's energy to feel appreciated, each will go lacking. Similarly, the masculine energies want to feel appreciated for their contributions, while feminine energies want to feel understood and appreciated for who they are.

I know...As a man I went from cold and distant to open and honest when things my wife said, made me feel that my skills and opinions are important and valid. A feminine woman can go from tight and controlling to free and radiant once her partner makes her feel appreciated, needed, and loved. Both energies must stop expecting their partner to be something they are not, and instead appreciate everything that they bring to the relationship. According to my wife with regards to polarity of difference. Substitutes "your expectations for appreciation, as a result your whole world changes. If your relationship is lacking polarity, you can learn how to get it back. If you're single and still searching for your husband or wife, learn and understand what type of energy you bring to a relationship and what you attract in return. "You can only get what you sow" Once you're clear in your purpose and recognize what's gone wrong, you'll discover how to use relationship polarity to feel fulfilled long-term. Arguably… Love is never free. There is always a price to pay for what each partner gives. People newly in love joyfully care for each other in every way they can. They strive to fulfill each other's every desire, and even attempt to anticipate them in advance. Their "generosity coffers" are overflowing, and they easily forgive when disappointments emerge. It's hard to look at the current state of your relationship, and questioned... is it truly all it could be right now? I had to ask this question constantly because I realized it was a daily walk that would only get better ...if I got better not my wife. If both you and your partner want to make this partnership work, what's preventing you from doing so? I had to release and knock down the walls I built up over time with my wife and gain an understanding of why I do the things I do. Above all...I had to identify the issues that creates pain for my wife and take responsibility for my role in them. Only then can you stop causing pain and start creating pleasure. This means that restoration polarity in relationships comes when we examine the issues in your life that have caused depolarization. For example. Did a medical scare cause the partner with feminine energy to inhabit a more masculine role in the relationship? Was it a surprising affair that caused the masculine partner to feel unseen and insecure, traits more closely linked to feminine energy? Just because your relationship polarity has shifted, doesn't mean it can't be helped.

His love paid off and paved the way for fulfillment.

Our culture packages love in jewelry commercials, flower bouquets, and boxes of confections. Celebrities pair up and break up with such regularity that weekly magazines and gossip websites thrive on the intrigue. Contemporary romantic comedies promote an if-it-feels-good-it-must-be-love mentality that leaves many moviegoers feeling empty...especially when their real life can't compete. And maybe that's where you are. Maybe you feel dead to love. If so, perhaps it's because you've been swindled into thinking what love is. Love the kind that's real—doesn't come wrapped on Valentine's Day. It's not the momentary glow of a fresh relationship. It's not the reuniting of two characters in a sappy movie. All in all. Real love is explained in the Bible. Real love is selfless, sacrificial, and unconditional. Jesus reaffirms "No greater love has no one than this, that someone lay down his life for his friends". (John 15:13) By this we know love, that he [Jesus] laid down his life for us, and we ought to lay down our lives for the brothers. (1 John 3:16). In our self-indulgent world, a love so sacrificial and selfless may sound like some impossible idea...some unreachable gold standard of what love could be...but it's not. It really happens, and it happened for my wife and me. All in all, what our world calls love often comes conditionally. If you mess it up, it's gone. If you don't pay the cost, it evaporates. Real love endures, doesn't keep a record of wrongs, doesn't seek its own and never fails (1 Corinthians 13:4–7). All things considered. He gave up more riches than you could imagine coming on a rescue mission. Although he didn't deserve it, he was betrayed, whipped, and beaten to fulfill that mission. Soon after, he died by one of the most painful forms of execution that humans have ever invented. He loved us and "gave himself as a ransom for all" (1 Timothy 2:6). In conclusion He lived entirely without sin, yet he walked up a hill in Israel 2,000 years ago and sacrificed his life to save sinners from God's wrath...the punishment we deserve for our rebellion (Romans 5:9). He didn't put stipulations on his love, (Romans 5:8) or only caring for the best of mankind (1 Corinthians 1:26). He went all in because he wanted to save us. Three days later, Jesus rose to life just as he predicted, proving he is the Son of God (Matthew 12:40; Revelation 1:18). He proved that he can indeed give us new life. In summary...For God so loved the world that He gave His only begotten Son, that whoever believes in Him should not perish but have everlasting life. (John 3:16, NKJV)

Chapter 28

The Intermittent Intent of Love

Below, you find…Whatever the specifics of our intention for love, it is a focus on what is important to us now and what we want to experience in the future. Intentionality is an important practice that, with understanding and dedication, can bring beneficial change to our lives. For one thing, intentions take work. We do not just wish things to be, they must be intentional. Along those lines, these four simple letters spell a very important word, love. The most eloquent of us, from John Keats to Carrie Bradshaw, have stumbled over the word as love. We all have experienced it in one form or another, and have set our intention to love, in hopes of avoiding stumbling blocks of loneliness and divorce. Whether we are entering into new relationships, or refreshing old ones, we have a vision of what they will be. We might want to set the course in a new direction or bring in someone who does not replicate the problematic situations of previous relationships. Whatever the specifics of our intention for love, it is a focus on what is important to us now, and what we want to experience in the future. Nevertheless…Intentionality is an important practice, which can bring beneficial change with understanding and dedication to our lives, when we realize its intentional. We do not just wish things into being. We must purposely set our mind to a goal with intention, then we identify and practice the things that will support with intention. Conversely…to practice intention without attachment means creating and holding an intention without becoming attached to a specific manifestation of the outcome of that intention. Setting an intention for love is no different. What you need to know about setting an intention for love is that you will still stumble in love (or out of it) despite your best intentions, and that's ok. No amount of love will save us from seeing what we need to see, and learning what we need to learn in relationships. No matter how awkward or painful, some lessons are only learned through experience. According to…Roman 5:1-4 Therefore being justified by faith; we have peace with God through our lord Jesus Christ: By whom also we have access by faith into this grace wherein we stand and rejoice in hope of the glory of God. And not only so, but we gory in tribulations, also: knowing that tribulation work patience; and patience, experience, and experience hope. It is possible that you can learn how to be more loving with yourself and others; through the ebbs of life regardless of your intention for love manifests itself, you will at least gain clarity, understanding, and conviction. If you are ready to open yourself up to bring love into your life, you should be happy and proud of your assuredness in doing so. Know that Love is a journey, not a destination. Therefore, use the following to help you set your intention on love.

Be clear: I can't tell you how many people I have heard say, "I made a list of exactly what I wanted in a partner, and I met him/her! It is uncanny how he/she is everything on the list." It is true that if you are clear about what you want, you will find it. So, go ahead! Make your list, and make sure it includes everything you can think you want.

Be open to more: The flip side to the list exercise is the reality that we don't know what we don't know. Your most detailed list of the traits you know you want in a partner won't include the traits you didn't think of – which might be wonderful – or the traits you've never encountered – which might be challenging. We want to be open to what is in our highest and best interest, regardless of whether we are consciously aware of it or not.

169

Hold onto the feeling: The best way to stay on track with an intention is to connect with the feeling that is associated with this intention. By connecting and reconnecting with this feeling, we are strengthening our process and intensifying our result. If we become doubtful or hopeless, it is this feeling that will help us stay the course.

Get rid of the baggage: It is hard to get something you do not feel like you deserve. If you have unresolved emotions or negative beliefs that are holding you back from being free and clear to get what you want, I suggest you do what is necessary to get them out of the way. A Breakthrough session with someone can be helpful in this regard. However, you want to pay attention to when and where negative emotions and beliefs show up after you set your intention. This will help you open and receive what you truly want.

Remain unattached: To get what you really want you can't get sidetracked by everything that is almost what you want. This means that when presented with an option that falls short, you acknowledge the shortcoming and let it go, holding your intention for what you truly want. It also means that when something comes your way, you both accept that it might be what you are truly looking for and give it the space and time to be what it truly is.

Learn to receive: We can be as intentional as we can be, but unless we learn to receive, our intention will not come to fruition. Receiving is an art that can be practiced. If you think that you might be challenged in this area, then start small. Start receiving compliments, gifts, and well-wishes as completely as you can. This practice will help you get more of whatever you want in your life, including love. In the past I did the exact opposite of what I am suggesting. Once I realized that, I needed to understand my vibrations and acknowledge my short coming. The was love. I was able to evolve into love and express love authentically.

Chapter 29

Intermittent Potential

Pursuing your full potential seems like a worthy goal, but it can also feel unrealistic and frustrating. Perhaps the most  reasonable aspiration is to realize more of our potential by finding the most gratifying pathways toward our best possible futures. The pathways to flourishing open when lower-level needs are satisfied in the moment and over time. The foundation of security, and therefore a requirement for sustained flourishing, is access to resources…physical and psychological, financial, medical, social, and natural/geographical…sufficient to pursue one's higher-level motives. Unfortunately, I did not understand that my life required heat, and pressure for change to take place. Nevertheless…The following are intermittent interludes of events; that became the catalyst to change. I literally had to reminiscence the mental and physical pain of my past before I was led into the wilderness of Egypt March 15th, 2019. As mentioned, my life as a child was filled with a lot of mental and physical abuse. The Paradox of events were confusing, yet comforting, truly unexplainable, despite that; I was led into the desert of Egypt for ten days. The polarity of difference is the pathway to flourishing freedom, when lower-level needs are satisfied in the moment and over time. The foundation of security, and therefore a requirement for sustained flourishing, is access to resources…physical and psychological, financial, medical, social, and naturally become sufficient to pursue one's higher-level motives. What took place as a child into adulthood really left me with a lot of uncertainties, questions and perplexation concerning who I was. All too often things appeared to be good but were all too disturbing. At my lowest point in life, I wanted to commit suicide; but God had seemingly touched me, and the touch was in every facet of my life despite the circumstance. While debatable, these are the facts, and because of what was happening to me as a teenager, I dropped out of school in the ninth grade. As a result, my body's alarm system, brain, and nervous system; experiencing chronic pain, my alarm system stayed turned on or was triggered to turn on. My brain and nervous system were trying to protect me from danger or a threat at hand. But with chronic pain and many other chronic health conditions, it is just not true. It's a false alarm. It's like a fire alarm going off without a fire. Research suggests ...we don't realize our brain and nervous system can get stuck in protection mode when current and past mental, emotional, or physical traumas or stresses (dangers) have not been resolved. The brain and nervous system also become more sensitized with every stress that occurs in your life and the longer you've had your condition the more sensitive and reactive it becomes to protect you from what it perceives as dangerous. In essence, the brain and nervous system become conditioned to overprotect you. Overprotection over time results in a host of physical health conditions and symptoms that don't go away. The keys to my success were to understand, accept, and realize that what happened to me as a child did not originate with me but originated from an outside source. I had exhale and make myself at home with Christ. As a result, I was able to cast down every evil imagination and every high thing that exalted itself against the knowledge of God and bringing down into captivity every thought to the obedience of Christ. For this reason, I had to sound the alarm about the mental health of children and what happened to me and so many children in our communities. It took the acknowledgement of every trial and tribulation, the fears, the struggles of pain, suicide, loneliness, rejection of failed relationships to get to this place of peace and acceptance.

172

The Polarities opposites or "opposition in all things:" Undoubtably comes with some hesitation. And because of the intercession for all, all men come unto God; wherefore, they stand in the presence of Christ, to be judged according to the truth and holiness which is in Him. Wherefore, the ends of the law which the Holy One hath given, unto the inflicting of the punishment, which is affixed, which punishment that is affixed is in opposition to that of the happiness, which is affixed, to answer the ends of the atonement for it must needs be, that there is an opposition in all things. If not so, my firstborn in the wilderness, righteousness could not be brought to pass, neither wickedness, neither holiness nor misery, neither good nor bad. Wherefore, all things must needs be a compound in one; wherefore, if it should be one body it must needs remain as dead, having no life neither death, nor corruption nor incorruption, happiness nor misery, neither sense nor insensibility. Wherefore, it must have been created for a thing of naught; wherefore there would have been no purpose in the end of its creation. Wherefore, this thing must needs destroy the wisdom of God and his eternal purposes, and the power, and the mercy, and the justice of God. And if ye shall say there is no law, ye shall also say there is no sin. If ye shall say there is no sin, ye shall also say there is no righteousness. And if there is no righteousness there be no happiness. And if there is no righteousness nor happiness there be no punishment nor misery. And if these things are not there is no God. And if there is no God we are not, neither the earth; for there could have been no creation of things, neither to act nor to be acted upon; wherefore, all things must have vanished away. And now, my sons, I speak unto you these things for your profit and learning; for there is a God, and he hath created all things, both the heavens and the earth, and all things that in them are, both things to act and things to be acted upon. And to bring about his eternal purposes in the end of man, after he had created our first parents, and the beasts of the field and the fowls of the air, and in fine, all things which are created, it must needs be that there was an opposition; even the forbidden fruit in opposition to the tree of life; the one being sweet and the other bitter.

Consequently, the Lord God gave unto man that he should act for himself. Wherefore Verily I say unto you, he that is  ordained of me and sent forth to preach the word of truth by the Comforter, in the Spirit of truth, doth he preaches it by the Spirit of truth or some other way? And if it be by some other way it is not of God. And again, he that received the word of truth, doth he receives it by the Spirit of truth or some other way? If it be some other way, it is not of God. Therefore, why is it that ye cannot understand and know, that he that receives the word by the Spirit of truth receives it as it is preached by the Spirit of truth? Wherefore, he that preaches, and he that receives, understand one another, and both are edified and rejoice together. And that which doth not edify is not of God and is darkness. It is here that the eyes of my understanding were enlightened in determining how precious we are in the creation of things, similarly…How much pressure it takes to turn coal into a diamond. It's that duress of approximately 725,000 pounds per square inch, and at temperatures of 2000 – 2200 degrees Fahrenheit, a diamond will begin to form. The carbon atoms bond together to form crystals under this high pressure and temperature. Certainly, within this process we can understand that a diamond in its original state is black; with this understanding we have come to understand how trials and tribulation form and align us to His will. Inevitably this process lasted a few years. Enduring the heat and pressure, while discovering spiritual discipline, this sounds like an easy task to put into practice. Unfortunately… In my discovery, I learned we cannot obtain discipline in our own strength, there are too many anomalies that make it impossible to always be on guard. The understanding of discipline intentional aim has

174

a predestined focus that cannot be usurped. The commitment is agonizing, frustrating; during refinery of prayer, giving, fasting, solitude, journaling, and being still. You might ask the question? What's the purpose? To become disciples of Christ. Discipline envelopes discipleship, which requires us to study to show yourself approved unto Him... to stay focused on the motivations of our heart that is towards Christ. He doesn't want us to fall into the trap of legalism, imposes a set of manmade rules on oneself unto himself and using them as justification for our action, but rather a tool for refining oneself. No one wants to fall into the trap of antinomianism, whereby minimizing the importance of discipling. Based on my finding here are six reasons every man and woman in Christ ought to be devoted to their walk towards discipleship in Christ intentionally.

1. *We practice spiritual* disciplines so that we can enjoy God (Psalm 63, 73:25-28). When you read the book of Psalms, you don't come away thinking the psalmist was burdened with the responsibility of spiritual disciplines. The intake of prayer and giving were not tasks to be enjoyed. Rather, they were means by which the psalmist enjoyed the very presence of God. This should be our approach towards each other.

2. *We practice spiritual* disciplines for the purpose of godliness (1 Timothy 4:7-8). Paul called Timothy to "train" for the purpose of "godliness." No one accidentally slides toward holiness. No one naturally drifts toward holiness. We must train. We must be disciplined. In heeding the biblical calls for God's people to be holy, we must see the disciplines as a means of training. "Count it all joy husband and wife when you fall into diver's temptations, knowing this is the trying of your faith, but let faith have its mature work in you that you may be whole wanting nothing."

3. The book of Psalms assumes God's people will practice spiritual disciplines (Psalm 1,19,119). The book of Genesis assumes the existence of God, the book of Psalms assumes God's people will engage in spiritual disciplines. Psalm 1 assumes we will meditate on God's Word. Psalm 19 assumes we will desire God's Word more than gold or honey. Psalm 119 assumes we will memorize God's Word. The assumption is that we will do this together not alone.

4. *Jesus assumes* his people will practice spiritual disciplines (Matthew 6:1-18). Jesus talked about spiritual disciplines in the most famous sermon he ever preached, the Sermon on the Mount. Jesus assumes we will be people who love God with all our heart, pray, and love thy neighbor as thyself. There is no consideration given to the possibility that we simply will not do these things. Jesus just assumes we will practice these disciplines.

5. *Nothing great happens* without discipline. Concert pianists don't reach the pinnacle of their craft without discipline. NBA All-Stars don't bask in the limelight without discipline. Graduates don't walk across the stage without discipline. Nothing great happens without discipline. Consequentially, many hopefully assume something great will happen in their spiritual life without discipline. "And beside this, giving all diligence, add to your faith virtue; and to virtue knowledge; and to knowledge temperance; and to temperance patience; and to patience godliness; and to godliness brotherly kindness; and to brotherly kindness charity".

6. *Discipline leads* to freedom. The hours of piano practice may have seemed like drudgery, but the result in freedom to play complex pieces of music with each other will lead to harmony. The hours of running and weightlifting may have seemed like torture, but the result is the freedom to do what the rest of us only dream about. The hours of study and writing may have seemed like a prison, but the result is freedom to think great thoughts. For as a man think in his heart so will they be.

I don't know where you are spiritually, but I do know you can start today. Be intentional. If Bible reading is a struggle, start with 5 minutes a day. If prayer is a struggle, start with a journal where you can record the prayer requests of your family and friends. If meditation is a struggle, try to set aside a few minutes at the end of the day to reflect on God's Word. The spiritual disciplines are not always easy, hence the name "disciplines." The good news is that God gives grace to His people. God's grace moves us to the disciplines, and the disciplines enable us to experience God's grace. With regards to...the process of heat and pressure results in the formation of you; becoming one with yourself in Christ. The action of forming or being formed. The coming into being a structure or arrangement of something. The unity of husband and wife is a spiritual formation with a physical representation. This means the process of discipleship leads to the following:

- Knowing Self, God
- Development of Prayer life
- Walking in Righteousness
- Having Discernment
- Direction and Purpose
- Being a Disciple
- Becoming the Husband or the Wife God intended

The word of God further implies, He is the potter, and we are the clay, and that process sharpens our attentiveness to  God and helps us to be more and more like Jesus, in the power of the Holy Spirit. These practices are shaped by our temperament and personality type. Putting it all together... Intentional -- Discipleship is not simply someone learning about Christ. It is not accidental. It's intentional. It is not a function of the learning of the learner but of the teaching of the teacher. Someone must intend to do it. Impacting --Discipleship has not happened because a student is excited about or impressed by a teacher. Discipleship brings about a change in virtues, values, beliefs, and lifestyle. Personal --Discipleship is not covering material. Neither is it being part of a group (a class, congregation, family, etc.). Discipleship is one person dealing with another person personally. Christlike --Discipleship is not just a mentee modeling a mentor. The modeling must be moving in the direction of Christlikeness. Furthermore…discipleship is incarnational. Incarnational means in-the-flesh. ("Carnation" means "flesh." For example, chile-con-carne means chile with flesh. "Carnal" desires are fleshly desires, etc.) In-the-fleshiness is what God used to reveal Himself to us in the person of Jesus Christ (John 1:14 and 1 John 1:1). Christ's apostles continued the incarnational approach. Paul reviews his ministry with the Thessalonians by comparing himself to a nursing mother tenderly caring for her own children and giving them not only the Gospel but his own life (1 Thessalonians 2:7-8). So, discipleship is done in the flesh. It cannot be done via books or tapes or TV or speakers in auditoriums. All these things may be useful, but discipleship is being there. Most importantly, I learned Biblical discipleship invites personal discovery. A disciple must discover the truth for him or herself. The disciple's job, then, is to present truth that must be self-discovered. Jesus often presented things in such a way that people had to look beyond the obvious and make the effort to discover what He meant. In John 2 He threw the money changers out of the Temple. When challenged about it, He said, destroy this Temple and in three days I will raise it up (verse 19). He was referring to His own bodily resurrection but understanding that was not easy. In John 3 Jesus required Nicodemus to discover what it meant to be born again (verse 7). In John 4 the woman at the well had to discover what He meant by living water (verse 10).

In John 6 the disciples had to discover what it meant to eat His flesh and drink His blood (verse 53). Discipleship was never simply a matter of parroting back answers or learning a program. It required a faith and focus that led to self-discovery. In conclusion…Biblical discipleship is the act of one person intentionally impacting the life of some other person in the direction of Christlikeness (2 Timothy 2:2). And it comes with a heavy price tag. One of the differences between discipleship and mentoring is the cost involved. Jesus said, if anyone comes to Me; first sit down and calculate the cost (Luke 14:26-28). In this passage Jesus gave us two costs to count: The first is the cost concerning others. He said we must "hate" our family and those close to us. Hate is not the opposite of love: apathy is. Rather, it is a choice which prioritizes one over the other (Malachi 1:2-4). The second cost has to do with us. Jesus said we must hate our own lives (Luke 14:26) and lose ourselves for His sake (Matthew 10:39; see also Ephesians 5:29) When purpose is not known abuse is inevitable, therefore discipleship reasons, persuades, and gives evidence. Discipleship is not based on mysticism, emotions, or blind faith. Through Isaiah God told Israel, come now, and let us reason together (Isaiah 1:18). Concerning Paul's discipleship, we read that he was reasoning in the synagogue every Sabbath and trying to persuade Jews and Greeks (Acts 18:4). We also read that Paul reasoned with them from the scriptures, explaining and giving evidence that the Christ had to suffer and rise again from the dead (Acts 17:2-4). (See also Acts 19:8-10; 28:23-24.)

The Intermittent Gifts

Though I speak with the tongues of men and of angels, but have not love, I have become sounding brass or a clanging cymbal. And though I have the gift of prophecy, and understand all mysteries and all knowledge, and though I have all faith, so that I could remove mountains, but have no love, I am nothing. And though I bestow all my goods to feed the poor, and though I give my body to be burned, but have no love, it profits me nothing. Once I became aware of the touch for God, I then had to understand; what it meant to have these gifts and how to allow them to manifest in my life. The first was love suffers long and is kind; love does not envy; love does not parade itself, is not puffed up; does not behave rudely, does not seek its own, is not provoked, thinks no evil; does not rejoice in iniquity, but rejoices in the truth; bears all things, believes all things, hopes all things, endures all things. Subsequently love never fails. But whether there are prophecies, they will fail; whether there are tongues, they will cease; whether there is knowledge, it will vanish away. For we know in part, and we prophesy in part. But when that which is mature has come, then that which is in part will be done away. Even more important in my late fifties, I had to embrace that when I was a child, I spoke as a child, I understood as a child, I thought as a child; but when I became a man, I had to put away childish things. For now, we see each other in a mirror, dimly, but then face to face. Now I know in part, but then I shall know just as I also am known. And now abide faith, hope, love, these three; but the greatest of these is love. However, I wonder how much do we really understand the words regarding how we display love, do we just merely understand the emotional aspect of love? Nevertheless, with much submission and correction, as a man I began evolving in my understanding that love is as a verb. Something we display in action not a feeling. As a society we have been nurtured to believe a lot of things that aren't apparently true in nature. Just look at the life of Christ. The greatest king became a servant. How did we lose this valuable lesson? All we must do is look back at some of the great men to recognize that being a leader, father and man meant the opposite of what we currently display in our society and in our Churches. You see the kingdom of God is upside down.

ENTRAPPED

Trapped,
By what should not be.
Entrapped in my loneliness,
That only I can see.
Reaching out I tried and died in
The effort.
Oh! If you could see the tears, I've cried.
Reaching up towards the sun.
Watching and waiting a new day has
Begun midnight again and I must retreat.
Entrapped, I am with the thought of what
should not be – cannot stop....
The darkness invades me
Cannot free myself from the chains of this Loneliness, this
pain, and its desire.
FREE ME! FREE ME!
from it all; before the tapping
Of the rainfall.

Chapter 30

Touched Psychologically

The Affect

We experience the touch of God in our lives as intermittent – it is real and undeniable, but also, like a  physical touch, fleeting, transient. We may feel that touch in times of grief. I must conclude that, once I was enlightened, my prayers and desires changed. Reading the words of 1 Samuel 10:26 moved me to pray for a new touch from God. "And Saul also went to his house at Gibeah; and the valiant men whose hearts God had touched went with him. "What a wonderful thing to be touched in the heart by God. There is nothing unusual about the Hebrew word here (naga'). It is simply "touch" in the ordinary sense. God touched their hearts. The touch of God in the heart is an awesome thing. It is awesome because the heart is so precious to us—so deep and intimate and personal. When the heart is touched, we are deeply touched. When the heart is touched the core of our being is touched. When the heart is touched someone has gotten through all the layers to the center. We have been known. We have been seen. We have been pierced.

The dramatic account in Acts describing the descent of the Spirit upon the apostles at Pentecost takes us into the Upper Room, calls us to receive the Spirit ourselves. But the feast of Pentecost is only the beginning: the coming of the Spirit into our lives does not end on that day. More than twenty weeks of 'time after Pentecost' follow, and this long period reminds us that the Spirit continues 'to help us in our weakness'. 'For when we cannot choose words in order to pray properly,' Paul tells us, 'The Spirit himself expresses our plea in a way that could never be put into words'. He endearingly adds, 'God, who knows everything in our hearts knows perfectly well what he means (Romans8:26). Subsequently...in the polarity of difference we must understand that scriptures summarize the countless gifts of the Holy Spirit, gifts of life and healing, hope, love, and strength, from the standpoint of completeness or limitless perfection/maturity. These gifts are divine promptings, not tangible and visible in the physical sense, but experienced by all believers. The Spirit mediates between the visible and the invisible (wisdom), between chaos and meaning (understanding), between time and eternity (right judgment), light and darkness (courage), the known and the unknown (knowledge), truth and illusion (trust), and between mystery and materiality (awe and wonder). As the 'finger of God's right hand', the Spirit points to the meaning behind events, stirs a sudden recognition of what is and what might be, helps us to articulate unspoken pleas and yearnings... Arguably...the Spirit is not always gentle and peaceful, soothing, and restful; just as important the Spirit can come to disturb or to challenge oneself, to awaken and to confront. For instance, within the context of psychology, affect refers to the feeling's humans have. They are used to qualify and describe moods. This can range from normal, everyday feelings to harmful or unregulated feelings. The effect is our body's emotional indicator as to whether everything is going okay or if there is something wrong. Research on affect tends to analyze feelings that are intense, difficult to perceive, or highly visceral to gain a better understanding of their function and purpose within the brain and body system. Affects are typically judged by emotional responses such as facial expressions, vocal expressions (such as tone of voice or laughing), energy levels, eye contact, and body movements. I Inherently embraced this concept when seeking the spirit, becoming completely fascinated with understanding the word of God and connecting the sequences of events to a more enlighten fulfilling life, but more importantly to the objective of becoming a disciple in Christ.

Ponder this…

Spirituality gives a sense of well-being and boosts our brain with hormones that strengthen the immune system. Factors like stress and pressure can take a huge toll on the body. Practicing spirituality helps build positive thoughts and increases the functioning of the body. However, Christ wasn't overly concerned about of physical bodies, yet He talked about it in a manner that will help us to better understand.

We can see that we occupy all the following aspects to our being.

- Physical Body
- Emotional Body
- Mental Body
- Spiritual Body

All these bodies matter in the grand skim of life, however, only one will give you eternal life. Our behaviors are a direct result of the energy exchanges between our bodies and our environment. This 'environment' not only includes things outside of our body but also things that make up the body itself (organs, tissues, cells, etc.). Our mind is watching over your bodily functions as much as it's monitoring the external environment. Even the thoughts that you think are considered as 'environment' by the mind because it responds to them in a similar fashion as it does to the external environment.

1 Thessalonians 5:23 - And the very God of peace sanctify you wholly; and I pray God your whole spirit and soul and body be preserved blameless unto the coming of our Lord

Jesus Christ. All that we are becoming is wrapped up in us dressing ourselves daily in this. We can easily dress up for sport events, work, vacation etc... We do this without stressing about it because it's what we want to do and must do in some cases. Ephesians 6:11 Context Knowing that whatsoever good thing any man doeth, the same shall he receive of the Lord, whether he be bond or free. And ye masters, do the same things unto them, forbearing threatening: knowing that your Master also is in heaven; neither is their respect of persons with him. Finally, my brethren, be strong in the Lord, and in the power of his might. Put on the whole armor of God, that ye may be able to stand against the wiles of the devil. For we wrestle not against flesh and blood, but against principalities, against powers, against the rulers of the darkness of this world, against spiritual wickedness in high places. Wherefore take unto you the whole armor of God, that ye may be able to withstand in the evil day, and having done all, to stand. Stand therefore, having your loins girt about with truth, and having on the breastplate of righteousness. More specifically... we receive energy from our external environment via the five senses.

This energy (information) is processed by our mind and interpreted in a certain way. This interpretation often happens subconsciously unless a person has raised their level of awareness. The way we interpret this information determines what kind of emotions we experience and the actions we take. As I said before, our mind also receives information from our internal environment i.e., our body and from our thoughts. This explains why we feel the emotion of hunger and why even thoughts (and not just the circumstances) have the power to trigger emotions. I have come to acknowledge that... This threshold varies from person to person and from emotion to emotion. Once this threshold is reached, the extra energy of the emotions becomes unbearable, and we're forced to act. However, based on some circumstantial pressure, we're unable to act, nevertheless, we can still channel out the energy in other ways such as talking, singing, writing, and so on. Or we may end up suppressing our emotions, but ultimately, they must leak out, even if that happens via the dreams we have at night.

NEEDLESS PAIN

Awaken by her clock at 6 a.m.
I'm walking down the steps,
It's all so dim.
Sitting by the fireplace, the tingling begins.
What is it, I ask?
I stare towards heaven with outstretched hands.
I'm lonely and lost I know you see.
May pains are too, too much for me.
I've tried and tried to make it plain, but my effort just caused me more pain. I closed my eyes then fell into a trance.
reminiscing the enlightenment that brought
our paths together.
Why, oh why must I suffer when the bird glides effortlessly through the air, and the water bends around every stone and ravine.
Roses and daffodils
live in their glory –
So, why can't I find love in life.
Is it only at the … End?

Chapter 31

The Purpose

Gooden further explains that spiritual strength and courage are needed for our walk with Christ in spiritual warfare and  suffering. Those who would prove themselves to have true grace and must aim put on the whole armor of God, which he prepares and bestows. The Christian armor is made to be worn; and there is no putting off our armor till we have done our warfare and finished our course. <u>The combat is not against human</u>, nor against our own corrupt nature only; we must deal with an enemy who has a thousand ways of beguiling unstable souls. The devils assault us in the things that belong to our souls, and labor to deface the heavenly image in our hearts. We must resolve by God's grace, not to yield to Satan, but to resist him, and he will flee.

What does put on the whole armor of God mean? To put on the full armor of God is to apply all the Gospel to all your life, physically, emotionally, mentally, and spiritual. The whole armor is the expression of your full trust in God and what He has done for you through Jesus Christ. Gooden had to learn how to dress daily in this new concept. It had to be viewed just as important as the food he ate and the air he breathes.

The Seven Body Pieces

All emotions in essence are the impulses to act, the instant plans for handling life, that evolution has instilled in us. The very root of the word *emotion* is *motere* the Latin word which means 'to move', plus the prefix 'e' to connote 'move away' suggesting that a tendency to act exists in every emotion. In this way emotions are the primary source of human energy, aspiration, and drive, activating our innermost feelings and purpose in life, and transforming them to the things we think, to the values we live by. It was under the construct of my enlightenment of the polarity of differences that gave me insight into my own vises and how to break free from the chain that tried to bind me. My emotional instability or immaturity points to an individual's failure to develop the degree of independence or self-reliance that is seen in a normal adult, with consequent use of immature adjustive patterns and inability to maintain equilibrium under stresses, unlike most individuals who do not have these negative traits. Emotionally disturbed or unstable individuals represent lack of capacity to dispose of problems and irritability, needing constant help to accomplish day-to-day tasks. They also show vulnerability and stubbornness, looking at the same time for sympathy. They are conceited, quarrelsome, infantile, self-centered, and demanding sort of persons.

It may be that…however the saving power of Christ is able to set us free from what can seem like the impossible. The law of Moses was unable to save us because of the weakness of our sinful nature. So, God did what the law could not do. He sent his own Son in a body like the bodies we sinners have. And in that body God declared an end to sin's control over us by giving his Son as a sacrifice for our sins. More important…In John 8:36, Jesus said, "If therefore the Son makes you free, you will be free indeed." Christ has set us free! But what has He set us free from? Realizing the freedoms Jesus has given us helps us keep our focus on Jesus Christ and rejoice at what He has done for us. As a key reminder…Colossians 1:21-23 21 Once you were alienated from God and were enemies in your minds because of your evil behavior, v22 But now he has reconciled you by Christ's physical body through death to present you holy in his sight, without blemish and free from accusation—I appeal to you therefore, brothers, by the mercies of God, to present your bodies as a living sacrifice, holy and acceptable to God, which is your spiritual worship. Do not be conformed to this world, but be transformed by the renewal of your mind, that by testing you may discern what is the will of God, what is good and acceptable and perfect. (Romans 12:1–2)

NOSTALGIC

Purple pictures painted skies.
As the moon stood there ever so near but far away.
Now and again, I look back and to
treasure moment without a trace.
The embrace. Nothing better than spending time with the
stars passing by in the cool breeze of winter.
It doesn't hurt to pretend, nostalgic by
The standing of time.
Now, has gone.
The present we hold, the future remains as it is.
Does it hurt to pretend?
My pain lingers on.
Painted pictures of now and then

Chapter 32

Intermittent Renewal of Your Mind

What does" Renewing of the Mind" Mean in the bible? Simply stated, renewing your mind according to Roman 12:2  means interpreting life through the lens of God's word and the inspiration of the Holy Spirit, rather than through the lens of your experiences, woundedness, trauma, preferences, or the opinions of others. The focus of Romans 12:2, "by the renewal of your mind." Do not be conformed to this world, but be transformed by the renewal of your mind, that by testing you may discern what is the will of God, what is good and acceptable and perfect." We are perfectly useless as Christ-exalting Christians if all we do is conform to the world around us. And the key to not wasting our lives with this kind of success and prosperity, Paul says, is being transformed. "Do not be conformed to this world but be transformed. "That word is used one time in all the gospels, namely, about Jesus on the mountain of transfiguration (the mountain of "transformation" same word, metemorphōthē) "And he was transfigured before them, and his face shone like the sun, and his clothes became white as light" (Matthew 17:2; Mark 9:2).

Its More Than External Transformation

Consequentially… nonconformity to the world does not primarily mean the external avoidance of worldly behaviors. That's included. But you can avoid all kinds of worldly behaviors and *not* be transformed. "As His face shown like the sun, and his clothes became white as light!" The same transformation is attracted to us spiritually, morally, and

190

mentally. The first encounter happens on the inside, the later at the resurrection i.e. The outside. So, Jesus says of us, at the resurrection: "Then the righteous will shine like the sun in the kingdom of their Father" (Matthew 13:43). "We are perfectly useless as Christians if all we do is conform to the world around us. "Transformation is not switching from the to-do list of the flesh to the to-do list of the law. When Paul replaces the list — the works — of the flesh, he does not replace it with the works of the law, but the fruit of the Spirit (Galatians 5:19–22). We are however commissioned to:

- Dress ourselves daily in Truth
- Put the Breastplate of Righteousness on daily!
- Dress with our Sandals of Peace
- Gird ourselves with the Shield of Faith
- Put on the Helmet of Salvation
- Dress ourselves with the Sword of The Spirit

These' bodily functions operate as one unit independent of the others. Similarly with our body and everything under the skin, the brain, the organs, and everything between the ears. It is the skeletal system, fascia, organs, and blood, veins, and ligaments. We usually know when our physical body is full or not, hurt or not, happy, or not, healthy, or not. The signs are visible and generally recognizable. It represents our physical experience in the world, our physiology, and our ability to heal. The Christian alternative to immoral behaviors is not a new list of moral behaviors. It is the triumphant power and transformation of the Holy Spirit through faith in Jesus Christ — our Savior, our Lord, our Treasure. "God has made us sufficient to be ministers of a new covenant, not of the letter but of the Spirit. For the letter kills, but the Spirit gives life" (2 Corinthians 3:6). So, transformation is a profound, blood-bought, Spirit-wrought change from the inside out. In the book of Romans 12:2, Paul now focuses on the essential means of transformation... "the renewal of your mind." "Do not be conformed to this world but be transformed by *the renewal of your mind.*" If you long to break loose from conformity to the world, If you long to be transformed and new from the inside out, If you long to be free from mere duty-driven Christianity, If you long to offer up your body as a living sacrifice so that your whole life becomes a spiritual act of worship and representation worthy of Christ above the worth of the world; then give yourself totally to pursuing this — *the renewal of your mind.* Arguably it is the key to transformation. "Do not be conformed to this world but be transformed by *the renewal of your mind.*" There are many who think that the only problem with the human mind is that it doesn't have access to all the knowledge it needs. So, education becomes the great instrument of redemption…personal and social. If all we get is more education, we would not use our minds to invent elaborate scams, and sophisticated terrorist plots, and complex schemes for embezzling, and fast-talking, mentally nimble radio rudeness. If people just got more education! The Bible has a far more profound analysis of the problem. In Ephesians 4:23 Paul uses a striking phrase to parallel Romans 12:2. He says, "Be renewed in the spirit of your minds." Now, what in the world is that? "The spirit of your mind." It means the human mind is not a sophisticated computer managing data, which it then faithfully presents to the heart for appropriate emotional responses. The mind has a "spirit." And we call it a "mindset." It doesn't just have a view; it has a viewpoint. It doesn't just have the power to perceive and detect; it also has a posture, a demeanor, a bearing, an attitude, a bent. "Be renewed in the *spirit* of your mind."

Unfortunately, "The problem with our minds is not merely that we are finite, but that we are fallen." and don't have all the information. A body that has a spirit, a bent, a mindset that is hostile to the absolute supremacy of God. Our minds are bent on not seeing God as infinitely more worthy of praise than we are, or the things we make or achieve. This is what we see in Romans 1:28, "Since they did not see fit to acknowledge God, God gave them up to a debased mind." This is who we  are by nature. We do not want to see God as worthy of knowing well and treasuring above all things. You know this is true about yourself because of how little effort you expend to know him, and because of how much effort it takes to make your mind spend any time getting to know God better. Clearly... The Bible says we have "exchanged the glory of the immortal God for images resembling mortal man" (Romans 1:23). And the image in the mirror is the mortal image we worship most. That's what's wrong with our minds. This illumines the relationship between verses 1 and 2 of Romans 12. Verse 1 says that we should present our bodies...that is, our whole active life...as a living sacrifice which is our spiritual service of *worship*. So, the aim of all life is worship. That is, we are to use our bodies...our whole lives... to display the worth of God and all that he is for us in Christ. Now it makes perfect sense when verse 2 says that, for that to happen, our minds must be renewed. Why? Because our minds are not by nature God-worshiping minds. They are by nature self-worshiping minds. That is the spirit of our minds.

The self-diagnoses...is, we know in part and therefore we see in part...God suggest to us to be renewed in our thought; let's consider the way Peter describes our mind-problem in 1 Peter 1:13–14, "Prepare...your *minds* for action...Do not be conformed to the passions of your former ignorance." There is an ignorance of God...a willful suppression of the truth of God (Romans 1:18) ...that makes us slaves to many passions and desires that would lose their power if we knew God as we ought (1 Thessalonians 4:5). "The passions of your former ignorance." Paul calls these passions, "deceitful desires" (Ephesians 4:22). They are life-ruining, worship-destroying desires, and they get their life and their power from the deceit of our minds. There is a kind of knowledge of God…a renewal of mind…that transforms us because it liberates us from the deceit and the power of alien passions. The other biblical diagnosis is in Ephesians 4:17–18, "You must no longer walk as the Gentiles do, in the futility of their minds. They are darkened in their understanding, alienated from the life of God because of the ignorance that is in them, due to their hardness of heart. "Paul takes us deeper than Peter here. He penetrates beneath the "futile mind" and the "darkened understanding" and the willful "ignorance" and says that it is all rooted in "the hardness of their heart." Here is the deepest disease, infecting everything else. Our mental suppression of liberating truth is rooted in the hardness of the heart. Our hard hearts will not submit to the supremacy of Christ, and therefore our blind minds cannot see the supremacy of Christ (see John 7:17).

The difficulty of ever achieving anything in life is the inability to accept oneself and to own your own mess. When I put away childish thinking, I gained access to being intermittently changed into the man in Christ. The declaration of James 5:16, "therefore, confess your sins to one another and pray for one another, that you may be healed". The prayer of a righteous person has great power; it leads to healing and restoration, attributes that are worth seeking. We are adopted into the family of God when we freely receive the gift of salvation; and God has purposefully placed us in families and communities because He knew it is not good for us to be alone. Our oneness is part of Gods eternal plan, and the only way to walk in our purpose is to persevere in laying down every weight and the pursuits of sin to follow Christ. "And I tell you, everyone who acknowledges me before men, the Son of Man also will acknowledge before angels of God, but the one who denies me before men will be denied before angels of God" Luke 12:8-9. Arguably…Forgiveness is important to God! We have been forgiven, and so we must lend that same forgiveness to each other. The intermittent touch of forgiveness comes from the spirit of God…it is real and undeniable, but also, like a physical touch, fleeting, transient. We may feel that touch in times of grief; in moments of unexpected attentiveness, when our minds are at peace and open to creative insight; or in times of questioning and bewilderment. The Spirit blows where it will, truly comes to us, but does not linger. The sudden encounter, the flash of inspiration or intuition, the connection made, these are signs that the Spirit has been with us, guiding us, enlightening us. All that is needed is our response: to allow the breath of the Spirit to transform us, to renew our minds in the face of the earth. Subsequently…Unless a Christian learns to renew their mind, they will continue to walk in defeat, struggle, and confusion, as they desire to experience a Spirit-led life yet, have no understanding of how or tools with which to see that life manifest. This is the predicament of most believers who live lives of religious obedience and obligation yet void of any real Spirit-led power. Without renewing your mind, the only two options are to wait, hope, and beg God to change you or to work, sweat, and strive on your own to achieve the results you so long to experience. Neither is God's best. Renewing your mind aligns your mind with the truth of God's Word by learning to recognize the lies of the enemy, replace them with the truth of God's Word and then reinforce that truth every time the enemy comes at them with those same lies. In 2 Corinthians 10:5 ESV, God's Word teaches us that "We destroy arguments and every lofty opinion raised against the knowledge of God and take every thought captive to obey Christ…" Taking a thought captive literally means to capture or conquer that thought as you identify it and compare it to God's Word. Does this thought agree with God's promises over my life or not? If not, then I cast it away…rejecting its influence in my life and I plant in its place one of God's promises from His Word.

In the same way...2 Peter 1:3-4, the Bible says "His divine power has given us everything we need for a godly life through our knowledge of him who called us by his own glory and goodness. Through these He has given us His precious and magnificent promises, so that through them you may become partakers of the divine nature, now that you have escaped the corruption in the world caused by evil desires." Did you get that? It's through God's precious promises that we participate in the divine nature. Renewed thoughts resulting in new beliefs help you engage with God's plan for your life because thoughts fuel your beliefs. Godly Kingdom-Focused thoughts are great fuel for your godly beliefs, while ungodly, fear-driven lies and half-truths fuel ungodly beliefs. Renewing your mind is not just a spiritual process, but a *physiological* one as well. When you intentionally change the way, you think to align with God's Word, it literally creates new connections and pathways in your brain to make that process easier and more preferred over time. Through the process of *neuroplasticity*, your brain can literally be reconfigured to align with the truth of God's Word and thus create the solutions, strategies, and opportunities that best align with God's plan for your life. Remember, in Proverbs 23:7 KJV "For as he thinketh in his heart, so is he." Your thoughts (which ultimately create your beliefs resulting in your actions) literally create the boundaries of your life. If you want to experience a different life—the abundant life Jesus promised—you must learn to intentionally renew your mind.

Chapter 33

Becoming the Mature...Man

The pathway to healing from hurt...is getting to the source of a wound to heal it, is a healthy process but one that takes  great wisdom and care, both spiritually and psychologically. We must be so careful in whose lap we lay our burdens. We prayerfully need to consider who God has placed in our lives to bear them with ease, so they don't become their burdens also. Our faith in Christ grows as we find people to hold us accountable, and counsel us through strongholds of sin. The apostle Matthew wrote, "If your brother sins against you, go, and tell him his fault, between you and him alone. If he listens to you, you have gained your brother" (Matthew 18:15). Maturity in Christ allows us the strength to be honest about sin and provides us with the proper perspective to know what is appropriate to confess out loud to another person. In all we do, we are to bring glory to God. To do that we need to focus on our emotional being, our mental state, and our spiritual body, this tells the story of our hearts towards God. "Out of the abundance of the heart the mouth will speak, for out of the heart flows the issues of life.

Ponder this!

Out of our heart are the issues of life; issues imply both sources and springs as well as issues. The issues of life are the flowing means common problems, issues, and/or crises that happen to normal people living normal lives. These include Managing one's relationships so that they are healthy and functional, could be surviving disabilities, coping with grief, loss, and self-esteem issues, situations that an individual perceives an obstruction or issue in the way of their happiness or goals, problems and issues that interfere with your quality of life or ability to achieve life goals. (See John 4:14). Our heart is related to the sources of life, the springs of life, and the issue of life (Isa. 12:3). As a result, the remedy to how we obey is found in Romans 12:2, "Be transformed in the renewal of your mind." First, before we can do anything, a double action of the Holy Spirit is required. And then we join him in these two actions. The reason I say the Holy Spirit is required is because this word "renewal" in Romans 12:2 is only used one other place in all the Greek Bible, namely, Titus 3:5 where Paul says this: "[God] saved us, not because of works done by us in righteousness, but according to his own mercy, by the washing of regeneration and renewal of the Holy Spirit." There's the word "renewal" which we've seen is so necessary. And it is renewal "of the Holy Spirit." The Spirit renews the mind. It is first and conclusive his work. We are radically dependent on him. Our efforts follow his initiatives and enabling's.

Chapter 34

The Emotionally Touched Body

Personally, it took some years for me truly understand all the emotion, that had infiltrated my mind and the construct of  previous experiences really had me confused and unable to fully embrace my own identity, let alone my identity in Christ. The polarity of difference in the experiences with the paradox of shifting my mindset intermittently towards Christ was not a walk in the park. I had to accept, recognized, and understand the paradigm shift from the carnal mind to the mind of Christ. The ability to understand, use and manage my own emotions in a positive way to relieve stresses, and learn how to communicate effectively, empathize with others, overcome challenges, and defuse conflict took time. In this same way…The nervous system, hormones, touch, water…water release (tears), and water absorption. When trying to hold onto or control things too closely, our emotion releases that energy. How we are doing emotionally is represented by how calm or rough the waters are in our thoughts and our dream state.

In the same way…this represents the bridge between our physical and mental state of being, it is where our experience of the world is synthesized and interpreted. It represents our feelings and relationship to all things (i.e., how we react, interpret, and respond to situations and outside energies, particularly non-factual…like how someone looks at us in a certain way. The connection between the mental-emotional body is the reason why there are always different sides to a story or situation…if the bodies are unbalanced, those situations can be greatly misread and misunderstood. When balanced, it represents centering and acting from the heart space. Along these lines, it should show us how we behave when governed by the Spirit of Christ? Inclusive, empathetic, open, honest, less, or non-judgmental toward others, and generous with help. Therefore, having a desire to give without expecting or wishing to receive something in return. Similarly, cortisol, insulin, estrogen, progesterone, and testosterone will be more balanced and even, blood sugar is more regulated, the heartbeat even and slow, and blood pressure balanced. The body does not retain water, nor is the body over-dehydrated. Based on my finding, I knew and had to admit; I was living outside of being emotionally balanced, which led to being quickly aggressive, obsessive, irrational, extremely irritated, depressed, overly anxious, often with feelings of drowning or hopeless conclusion of relationships or situations. These behaviors can and will manifest into all kinds of physical trauma acting like a sponge, over-firing their nervous system, which also manifests as being underweight, dehydrated, or desiccated. Being in balanced are key to our overall health in Christ. Until now…I had not known that anything that releases emotion, tension, stress, and anxiety…will create clear, running waters with fewer rocks or less damning of the stream. Depending on the person this might require something like meditation, dance cardio, or breathing techniques. Ultimately, the emotional body comes into great balance when we learn how important it is to be in balance spiritually, mentally, and physical with ourselves through, meditating upon His word day and night, exercises, detoxing, or fasting and walking in the love of the cross as found in I Corinthians 13 chapter, which is the key regarding forgiveness which is also crucial. As explained once, I put away childish thinking …the man began learning the value of emotional intelligence but mental intelligence, which is central to empathetic and adrenal wellness.

Our Mental Body

Our bodies are so important that the Lord calls the temples of God 1Corithians 3:16-17; 6:19-21. Our bodies are important; our Father in Heaven wants us to take good care of them. He knows that we can be happier, better people if we are healthy. Its therefore can be concluded, that our thoughts, attitudes, judgments, and prejudices, shape how we perceive our worth and value in the world; and it represents all things intellectual, including analytical thought, how we process information, how we learn in school, and how we use our words...which includes focus, clarity, direction, and contributions to creation and society. It is a key element in thoughts becoming reality. It may be when the mental body is balanced, we become proactive problem solvers, concise communicators, innovations coming into fruition with clarity and ease, and the ability to solve emotional or physical issues in a direct and supportive way. Arguably... when the Spirit, Soul and body are working the way God intended there's very little waste, nonsense, or going around in circles. Instead, a balanced mental body offers direction that points true north (and benefits everyone). The polarity of difference in mentally unbalanced consequentially brings. Confusion, brain fog, ideas lost quickly, lethargy, lack of purpose, neuroses, doubt, a lack of work ethic, feelings of low esteem and low worth...which manifests physically.

In my past I was someone mentally overbalanced: Ego-centric, excessively driven, having little or no empathy, and frequently living in overdrive. As a result, it brought me to my knees to Christ on how to have balance. This led me to exercising, communicating with emotionally intelligent accountability with Christian partner, and being in touch emotionally and spirituality for balance. Hence, I was that person living mostly in the mental body overthinking everything and in constant overdrive and wouldn't let go of emotional strife or forgive easily or often. You can be set free; however, it will require working through old emotional pains with a mature emotional mentor who can lead you through positive thought mantras or positive stress releasing actions.

BUTTERFLIES

Butterflies come.
It is within life's battles we find the
Butterflies.
These butterflies that come, they come
To snare our soul; from whence we
Cannot ignore.
But there in the distance of these weary foes
Emerges a butterfly from beneath the snow.
From whence came thee and where shall I go?
For my eyes cannot envision because of the
Brightness of your glow.
Lead me, I ask to the field of a greener
Path. Look at my child for the butterfly.
Is it beyond your reach?
Take risk when you reach for the
Beautiful.
When you reach out for the finer
More fragrant things of life,
There is always a risk my child.
For life is exciting and awaiting you
With adventures bursting with butterflies.
Take the risk – the butterflies await you.

Chapter 35

The Paradox of our Spiritual Body

If there is a natural body, there is a spiritual body. Christian teaching traditionally interprets Paul as comparing a  resurrected body with a mortal body, saying that it will be a different kind of body, a spiritual body. Meaning an immortal or incorruptible body. Our spiritual body is the connection to all things, inclusive to all things in His creation the earth/self, beyond the universe, and the divine or higher self. This provides protection, union, help, and guidance from an outside source of this world. It connects us to all that is. We aren't inclined to understand or acknowledge this aspect exists. It has little to do with what we believe culturally when it comes to religion or spirit…it is more the element that no one and no situation stands alone, that there is power in the fact that we are all connected, and it always takes every member of the body to create all that exists in life. It is possible that the unity of all living things, including the union between our soul, life experience, and destiny, is not about going to church. In fact, it has little to do with religion, and everything you believe in Christ Jesus. According to Act 1:12 reflects how the power of His spirit behaves when balanced in one accord through being intermittently touched with being... calm, fearless, highly creative, and operating without limit…paired with the fortitude and support to create action from ideas. Thus, tamping into the wisdom and acknowledgement that there's a higher force guiding and protecting the purpose, and plan He has established before the foundation of the world. Our spiritual body represents the synthesis and balance of the Father, Son, and Holy Spirit. We are not greater than the sum of our parts. It may be the reason He states forsake not the assembling of yourselves as some have and have fallen away from the faith. This disconnecting of ourselves will lead to feeling or thinking that we can do things on our own or alone. That we are not co-creating our existence, that we are victims of fate (or the health care system, the government, or the media) and most often (or entirely) dismissive of listening to the spirit. This person generally separates from being an active or conscious member of community or society and feels deserving and expectant of others' energy or time. They also feel left out, or like they have not been seen or heard. There's also a tendency to put a high emphasis on how things look or how they appear instead of focusing on transparency and honest heart communication. There's also a heavy focus and over-reliance on doing, controlling, and the grasping of an exterior reference or relationship. This means you would be subjected to walking with your head in the clouds, having a false god complex, a lack of unity between action and behavior, a lack of connection to interpersonal responsibilities (relationships, physical health, and wealth, respecting other people's bodies, paying bills, debts). There is generally a feeling of entitlement and being overly deserving. Along these lines the scripture declares in Roman 12:3 because God is gracias to us; do not think of yourself more highly than you should.

It's your body, how will you dress yourself from this point forward?

Chapter 36

Preparations for the Conquest

The rules of the world are the beliefs of pagans. Gooden

 exclaimed that considering all the circumstances that have transpired over the last several years left us all asking these Questions:

- Does my life reflect the stresses of manmade rules and taboos rather than God's grace?
- Does it foster a critical spirit towards others, or does it exercise discipline, discreetly and lovingly?
- Does it stress formulas, secrets knowledge or special vison more than the word of God?
- Does your life elevate self-righteousness, honoring those who keep the rules rather than elevating Christs?

The storyline of this life lends me a hand in the universal circumstances that plagued us during the Covid outbreak. It was determined by some that the circumstances of the plague caused an awakening into who we thought we were; and what we believed. It revealed our inability to focus, mentally distorted, physically bored with ourselves, discontented with our spouses, and no joy or peace etc... We lost faith, hope, and love. God was an afterthought to many, and we seemingly just did not know who God was anymore because we did not really have the relationship, we thought we had. Similarly…we are entering into another abyss with circumstances where our true identities are being revealed. An adjustment is needed for us to be relevant and to reevaluate our personal perspective on life in lieu of our surroundings and those you think you are connected to and what is connected to you. Your connection points are indicators to your overall health, wellbeing physically and spiritually…. your vibration.

We are what we Eat.

After the death of Moses, the servant of the Lord, the Lord said to Joshua's son of Nun, Moses' aide: "Moses my servant is dead. Now then, you and all these people, get ready to cross the Jordan River into the land I am about to give to them-to the Israelites. I will give you every place where you set your foot, as I promised Moses. Your territory will extend from the desert to Lebanon, and from the great river, the Euphrates-all the Hittite country-to the Mediterranean Sea in the west. No one will be able to stand against you all the days of your life. As I was with Moses, so I will be with you; I will never leave you nor forsake you. Be strong and courageous, because you will lead these people to inherit the land, I swore to their ancestors to give them. "Be strong and very courageous. Be careful to obey all the law my servant Moses gave you; do not turn from it to the right or to the left, that you may be successful wherever you go. Keep this Book of the Law always on your lips; meditate on it day and night, so that you may be careful to do everything written in it. Then you will be prosperous and successful. Have I not commanded you? Be strong and courageous. Do not be afraid; do not be discouraged, for the Lord your God will be with you wherever you go."

Ponder this….

Once you do this expect your mind and desire to be transformed into the mindset of Christ. Let this mind that is in Christ be in you. Philippian 2:5. This announcement was an intermittent call to righteousness.

On the contrary... Gooden suggests that we are living in this make-believe life scenario pinned up on circumstances that appeal to our natural desires, which are in direct conflict to our predisposed purpose in Christ.

We have come to the realization that we have failed and refuse to admit it. We all are born and shaped in iniquity, drawn away from our own lust. Gooden concurs with James 1:14-15 that presents three statements that reveal a three-step process whereby sinful temptation and sinful behavior take hold upon our hearts and lives. Each of these three statements contains the relative conjunction "when," revealing a  conditional truth that when a certain event occurs, then a certain result will arise. First, verse 14 present lust and character of sinful temptation... "But every man is tempted, when he is drawn away of his own lust, and enticed.". Temptation comes from our own desires, which entice us and drag us away. But each one is tempted when, by his own evil desires, he is lured away and enticed. Gooden suggests that the temptation that lured him as a child became his vibrational match. Therefore, he was unknowingly becoming what was invested in his life. I had to want to change Gooden exclaims that meant I had to lay aside every weight and the sin that was so easily besetting him. Advising the practical encouragement in the third chapter of Colossians, which gives a series of admonitions in directing believers on how to successfully live the Christian life. They were in danger of being led astray by the deceptive doctrine of the false teachers who variously advocated philosophy, legalism, mysticism, ritualism, or asceticism as the means to produce a godly life. The word of God summarizes their teaching and practices, to having the appearance of wisdom in self-made religion and self-abasement and severe treatment of the body, [but are] of no value against fleshly indulgence." These teaching and practices of philosophy, ultimately fail in making a person right with God and in controlling fleshly desire. Why? Gooden suggest, because sin is a problem of the mind and heart and not just outward behavior. Self-discipline can result in restricting a behavior, but it cannot change the sinful heart, so sinful thoughts continue, and sinful behavior erupts in other areas. For this reason, we must mortify the flesh, however it cannot be conquered under the system of our original state of mind. Thus, the reasoning behind what Paul said in the previous verses is the reason for what he is about to command. In those verses we found that the real key to living in godliness is Christ. In just those first four verses Paul makes five references to Jesus – four by title and once by a personal pronoun. We are raised up with Christ (vs. 1); sit where Christ is (vs. 1); have our life hidden in Christ (vs. 3); and will be revealed with Him (vs. 4) when Christ, who is our life, is revealed (vs.4). It is our identification with Jesus' death (vs.3), resurrection (vs. 1), life (vs. 3 & 4) and glory (vs. 4) that is the basis for Paul's command here to "consider the members of your earthly body as dead to immorality, impurity, passion, evil desire, and greed, which amounts to idolatry." That is why… being intermittently touched by Christ through the holy spirit is so important to the adjustment of our thoughts. Undoubtedly… like many; I had no idea how important the heart and mind played into the overall productivity of life until the word of God revealed it. Everything you touch can be a vibration and therefore can infiltrate you from the eyes, mind, ears, and heart. Paul lists five specific elements that are part of our earthly members that he states that we are to put to death. Since some of these are not physical, we know that these "members which are on the earth" also encompass your mind and will. Your old self or old man (Colossians 3:9) is more than just your physical body, but also includes your old way of thinking and what you desire, which is why our minds must be renewed (Romans 12:2). These five deeds and desires are only representative since Paul includes a second list in verses 8 and 9, and passages such as Galatians 5:19-21 list out many more specific sins. We also find that this list moves from  physical actions to the motives that led to those actions…immorality, impurity, passion, evil desire and finally, greed. The issues surrounding sins of immorality are a problem today just as they were in the ancient world, therefore the same admonitions and corrections apply. The Jerusalem Council in Acts 15 issued a warning that the Gentile believers avoid immorality. The attitude in Corinth was so bad that some of the believers there were still consorting with the temple prostitutes. Paul had to strongly correct them that in doing so they were joining Christ to a harlot, and so they needed to flee immorality and glorify God with their bodies (1 Corinthians 6:12-20). Unfortunately, we are living in a society that is increasingly sexually perverse and open about it. Tragically, so many have fallen into this sin that fornication and adultery are considered normal with homosexuality not far behind in its acceptance.

The polarity of difference between my past and present life had to come to a crossroad. I had to accept my past but embrace my future… if I was to walk in Christ, I must recognize that I am a new creation. The old has passed away; behold the new has come. However, in that posture I cannot consider myself as one who has made it on my own. But one thing I do; forgetting what's behind me and persevering to what lies ahead, I therefore press towards the goal for the prize of the upward call of God in Christ Jesus. Philippians 3:13-14. Generally, speaking, the scriptures are always humbling and encouraging. Every true Christian was previously "a child of wrath" that was dead in trespasses and sins, walking according to the course of this world, living in the lusts of the flesh, and indulging the desires of the flesh and of the mind (Ephesians 2:1-3). We did not save ourselves by any sort of righteous deeds which we have done, since we are all as filthy rags before our Holy God (Titus 3:5; Isaiah 64:6). Instead, it was God's love demonstrated to us while we were yet sinners (Romans 5:8) that extended His mercy and grace to save us by the washing of regeneration and renewing by the Holy Spirit (Titus 3:5) and justifying us before Him on the basis of faith in the person and work of Jesus Christ in His atonement for our sin (Romans 3:28; 5:9). The result of salvation in Jesus Christ is that we become new creations in Him (2 Corinthians 5:17) who have been bought with the price of Jesus' blood so that we are not our own (1 Corinthians 6:19,20; Ephesians 1:7). We have been adopted in the God's family so that we can call Him "abba" (John 1:12; Romans 8:15), yet the reality is that we have also been bought so that we are God's bondservants…actually, slaves (1 Peter 2:16).

THE TAPPING OF THE RAIN

It was but an hour into the day,
Before the rain came dripping my way.
A drop here and a drop there,
Oh, what sudden despair.
Gazing out of this window, I stare
Alone without a care.
When will it stop and where shall I go?
Can you stop the rain from falling?
Can you stop the drowning of my tears?
Upon the window of my soul?
The tapping of the rain, left without
A trace.
The tapping of the rain.
Upon the window of my soul.

Chapter 37

Touched to be a Servant

The words touched to be a servant carries with it the polarity of difference in the paradox of servanthood.  Historically over 2000 years ago this word had to be unsettling. That because this statement by Jesus underscore's one of the great paradoxes of Christian faith…we lead by serving. Whoever wants to be great must be a servant. The greatest among you shall be your servant. Mark 9:35 Sitting down, Jesus called the Twelve and said, "If anyone wants to be first, he must be the last of all and the servant of all." Mark 10:43 But it shall not be this way among you. Instead, whoever wants to become great among you must be your servant. Based on my finding before moving on, I discovered; we see unseen things, we conquer by yielding, we find rest under a yoke, we reign with Him by serving others, we are made great by becoming small, we are exalted when we are humble, we gain strength when we are weak, we triumph through defeat, we find victory by glorifying in our infirmities and we live by dying. Thus, the reason   to really grasp servant and to accept the holy spirit. The reason Christ discusses the importance of grasping an understanding what we supposed to be following as a new believer. Christ set the ultimate example by giving up heaven, taking on human form, and living among us. He loved even more those who rejected Him. That's what it means to be a servant leader.   According to Mark 9:35, Jesus called the Twelve and said, "If anyone wants to be first, he must be the last of all and the servant of all." Mark 10:43 But it shall not be this way among you. Instead, whoever wants to become great among you must be your servant. The Greek "Servant" is a translation of the Greek word doulos, which means more literally "a slave or bondservant, someone who sets aside all rights of his own to serve another." Because the word slave carries such a negative connotation to our modern sensitivities, we often choose the word servant instead. Hence... the concept of servant leadership takes an altruistic approach to leading by focusing on the support and growth of others. A true servant leader is a servant first, serving others to not only help produce quality results but to improve their professional growth as well (whereas leader-first roles are usually more about power and acquisition of control).

A servant leader focuses more on involving all members rather than a more authoritative, traditional leader would. Servant leadership skills help connect the body to all members of the body on all levels to build the body as an efficient, synergistic engine. The idea of servant leadership encompasses many qualities beyond "the servant as leader." Some of the key characteristics of servant leaders include:

Strong decision-making skills: The servant leadership philosophy emphasizes people's needs. A good leader still must use their knowledge and experience to make a conscious choice to benefit the purpose of Christ and not this self-absorption of ego, and it may not always be an easy choice. However, a strong servant leader reflects the characteristics of Christ. It's an unpopular decision when so many of their peers are standing on the same block.

Emotional intelligence: Church leaders Must be the servant leader that pays attention to and understands the needs of others of Christ above their own for the body of Christ. A great leader listens well and takes the perspectives and experiences of others into account.

A sense of community: Building community is important for the body of Christ is a shared environment. An environment that supplies and nourishes each other.

Self-awareness: A rounded understanding of various approaches requires self-awareness. Consciousness of how your own behavior affects those around you is essential. Managing emotions and behavior, especially during critical moments, is key to establishing trust and openness among every member of the body.

Foresight: A servant uses their past experiences to inform them about the future. They can think ahead and see the likely outcomes or consequences of potential actions. Servant also knows when to follow their instincts based on the knowledge, they've gained over the years but rely on the Holy Spirit and the experience of those God has joined to the body of Christ.

Commitment to others: The servant model must reflect the humility and character of Christ and not their own agenda, but the development and well-being of others. The more efficient each member of the body becomes the more powerful we are as a body. It is important for all believers to take the posture of servant. The servant feeds every part of the body for personal growth.

Therefore… Now that I, your Lord, and Teacher, have washed your feet, you also should wash one another's feet. I have set you an example that you should do as I have done for you. Very truly I tell you, no servant is greater than his master, nor is a messenger greater than the one who sent him. Now that you know these things, you will be blessed if you do them.'(John 13:14-17), following the Lord Jesus' example of servant leadership in this passage, let us consider the characteristics of servant leadership, which he revealed and demonstrated as a commission for every believer. This means…love or compassion can be defined as seeing a need and lovingly doing something about it. What needs did Jesus  see? The disciples' dirty feet that need washing. Their psychological need the evening when they were going to Gethsemane, so Jesus gave them a foot spa? The need for tender loving care? Might Jesus be concerned about pride which can endanger the body of Christ if the head and hands tell the heart and feet that they are not needed? Did Jesus see all those needs and perform this humble act to meet the needs lovingly? 1 Corinthians 13 tells us that love is patient and kind. It does not envy. It does not boast. I am not proud. Practicing compassionate leadership means listening with fascination to those we lead, arriving at a shared (rather than imposed) understanding of the challenges we face. It is about empathizing with and caring for the team, taking action to help and support them. How can we love and pray for our teams? Can we do more than making coffee for the team after a ward round?

Other-centered: Servant leadership is characterized by humility (a willingness to listen and learn from criticism). Did you notice how Jesus gave space and time to Peter? When Peter asked him those silly questions, he didn't say to Peter, 'Come on, let's just get on with it. We must go to Gethsemane in a moment.' Should we encourage a less hierarchical team structure so everybody can voice their opinion and be valued? After checking the understanding of the team, we also need the courage to correct any misunderstanding and do the necessary. Jesus is an authentic leader (showing his true feelings). Servant leaders are also willing to forgive. We see the supreme example of servant leadership when Jesus washes his disciples' feet, an act of service only a slave was supposed to do. Jesus redefined leadership as serving each other in love, meaning there was no job that was low or demeaning to do.

Vision: Jesus always had a long-term, big picture vision. He knew what the Father had planned and walked the path towards the Cross every day of his earthly ministry. But his disciples could not grasp it. In all four gospels, Jesus explains what is going to happen to him time and time again, but none of his followers can get their heads around it. After his death and resurrection, it took him the whole walk from Jerusalem to Emmaus to explain to Cleopas and his companion how the whole of the Hebrew Scriptures pointed to the Cross and the resurrection as God's plan for salvation. It was then that the penny finally dropped, and they rushed back to Jerusalem to tell the others.

A visionary leader does not just have a vision. They take the time to share it with their team, in different ways, at different times, until the whole team grasps the big picture and can articulate it to outsiders. But often, until they see it in practice, modelled by the leader, the team can find it hard to get the vision clear in their heads. The visionary leads from the front. Always work for the good of the whole - making sure everything the team does serves the core vision. Servant leaders also show good stewardship, ensuring that all the resources the team uses are deployed as effectively and efficiently as possible to achieve the vision. Do you have a clear vision of what your team is there to do, a big picture of what it can achieve?

Empowerment: leading by example with clear instructions and appropriate delegation. Give your team responsibility and permission to exercise it. With permission to take on responsibility is permission to innovate and change, but also to fail safely. Failure must be seen as a chance to learn and develop confidence and skills. Are we committed to helping the team develop in this manner, especially when we must stretch our comfort zones? One of the things we need to persistently pray for is wisdom to manage uncertainty and for research efforts to improve understanding. Finally, in verse 17, Jesus said, 'Now that you know these things, you will be blessed if you do them.' Are we able to hold our team accountable and give credit where credit is due? The motivation that led Jesus to wash his disciples' feet. Verse three gave us an important clue- 'Jesus knew that the Father had put all things under his power, and that he had come from God and was returning to God.' Jesus was motivated by this eternal hope and everlasting love (verse 1). Thanks to Jesus' death on the Cross, taking our punishment for sins which separated us from God, we also have an eternal hope. Does that motivate us to be servant leaders and love and persistently pray for our teams? May the risen Lord Jesus pour out his Holy Spirit on his followers and empower us to be servant leaders. Let us take heed of Jesus' calling as he holds us accountable, 'Now that you know these things, you will be blessed if you do them'. (John 13:17)

ASHORE

I was a ship without a sail,
Buoyed on air without an end
In sight.
Then he walked out from the clouds,
Out of nowhere and drew ever,
So near.
I stopped and pinched myself …
Is this real?
My ship had landed on an island,
Nestled by birds of paradise and
All sorts of wisdom.
He enveloped me in the beauty of His love
Surrounded by peace and joy.
The strips that healed my soul, allowed my sails to come down, As I came ashore, now I know… I
Have been found.

Chapter 38

Your Potential Intermittently Unleash

Potential is one of the most dangerous words in the dictionary. If you achieve it, you're capable of greatness. But  missing it means you stay stagnant and frustrated. The antidotes to unleashing your potential and achieving and understanding your roles in Christ; lies with you shifting your thoughts into a new way of living, new way of thinking, new way of studying and of being is amongst the most complex paradigm shifts in the world today. Just as complex as finding a trusted teacher/counselor and Psychotherapist to aid your efforts.

- Jeremiah 29:11: "For I know the plans that I have for you,' declares the Lord, 'plans for welfare and not for calamity to give you a future and a hope."
- Galatians 5:5: "For we through the Spirit, by faith, are waiting for the hope of righteousness."
- Deuteronomy 11:26: "See, I am setting before you today a blessing and a curse."
- Ephesians 3:20: "Now unto him that is able to do exceedingly abundantly above all that we ask or think, according to the power that worketh in us."
- Philippians 4:13: "I can do all things through Christ which strengthened me."
- Luke 1:37: "For with God nothing shall be impossible."

We all live wanting to make our personal identity known, because it is of immense importance to us. Consider social media, we post all sorts of things as if it validates our mere existence, but all the while we struggle in the quietness of our heart asking, "Who am I?" and why do I Exist? Overall…this is not just a preteen question or something we struggled with when we were a junior in high school, trying to pick a college to attend. People in their thirty's, forty's, fifties, and sixties are still struggling to find their unique voice in the world; wandering around life trying to discover our true purpose. Trust me I know because I was that person in my twenty's thirties and late forty's; because even as a Christian I did not have all the necessary tools needed to fully understand who I was, or my real purpose and potential in Christ. Therefore, I was functioning as if I had amnesia searching for my identity. We eventually wake up and ask the age-old question, "WHO AM I?" I have done it. I have peered across the bathroom counter into the eyes in the mirror and asked, "Who are you and why do you exist? Great people in the Bible like David (2 Sam. 7:18), Ruth (Ruth 2:10) and Moses (Exodus 3:11) all asked comparable questions. Yet, once they understood their identity in God, nothing could stop them from living out their life purpose. Nothing! Knowing who we are in Christ begins with understanding who God is. Colossians 1:15-16 talks about Christ being the creator of all things. That by God, He created all things… including you! He does not make any accidents. He wires everything into our life, our gifting, our experience, our passion, all designed on purpose. Finding my life purpose required a right view of God and a right view of myself. I must see Christ for who He really is and know that He has plans greater than anything I could ever dream. Similarly, I must gain a perspective of who I am. I must understand the change in basic assumptions of things that have to be removed from my life, so that I can walk in a manner that pleases Him. I must also see that I have been designed in such a way that my unique purposes, passions, and aptitudes, can be used for His glory. We do not have to walk around with amnesia, forgetting our identity in Christ. We also do not have to look to others for approval. We must have the grace to accept that who we are is who God has intended for us to be;

218

getting rid of the things in our life that do not please Him, and walking fully into the life He has planned for each one of us. In conclusion…I had to accept the things that happened to me to be free to accept the path before me. The process to releasing your potential is a process is a series of action or step taken to achieve a particular end. God knew that some things had to happen to David's life before he could be king. Likewise, there are things that need to happen in our lives before we can step into what God has for us. Trust the process…God's plan for fulfilling His promises for your life is intermittent.

Consequentially… David could have quickly become bitter in his waiting; however, he perseveres instead of becoming bitter. Why? David knew that God was using the process to bring about God's promise for him to be king. Like many of us David could have easily gotten bitter and moved into unbelief and said for example "But, I had faith, and God didn't do it." And they're frustrated because they thought God said it would happen and it didn't. I *had* faith. This is a past-tense statement. This is not how faith works. If you think you can have faith in a moment, and have your faith go away when nothing happens in that moment, it's not faith at all. The Paradox in Faith is what keeps you going until you see God do what He has promised. Faith causes you to say, "I may not have seen it yet, but if God promised it, I am sure I will!" I had concluded despite what I had previously believed and went through and embrace that I will go through a process that God will use to bring about His promises, that will strengthen my faith. As a result, we get better instead of getting bitter.

Chapter 39

Anointed, Intermittently Not Appointed

It is God who established us with Christ, and has anointed  us, and who has also put His seal on us and given us His Spirit in our hearts as a guarantee. One of the things that seems to hinder a lot of Christian in our walk, is that they mistake the anointing of God for the appointing of God. Many are called but few are chosen. David had the anointing to be king, but he didn't yet have the appointment to be king. Sometimes, you can have an anointing in your life to do something, but not the appointment. As a young Christian this was one thing, I learned despite everything else, gifts are without repentance. Think about this: David could see the anointing. Other people could see the anointing. When Samuel poured the oil over his head and anointed him king, everyone was watching. The anointing moment is where it can get tricky. You can see your anointing; you're a better salesperson than anyone else, you're a great singer, you have influence, you can counsel, you can lead! And other people can see it, too. They tell you how talented you are, how great you are, and how far you will go! This can then cause you to think, "Well, I can see it, and others can see it, why can't God see it? What is God waiting for? "And through all of this and begin to focus on the light at the end of the tunnel that you can't see what's happening around you. Your eyes can't adjust to your surroundings because all you can see is the light up ahead and so you miss things, or you find yourself tripping over things because you can't see! If you can't see what God is doing in and around you because you are focused on a future dream, you can miss out on a lot of learning experiences and opportunities along the way. We can see this in Roman 5:3-4 Therefore being justified by faith; we have peace with God through our lord Jesus Christ; by whom also we have access by faith into his grace wherein we stand and rejoice in the hope of the glory of God. And not only so, but we glory in tribulations; knowing that tribulation works patience; and patience, experience; and experience hope.

Intermittent Preparational Key

After his anointing, David's appointment was to watch the sheep. Sometimes, we think that watching is just something we do to pass the time until we can do what we're supposed to do, but that's not the case. If you're watching the sheep right now,. you're supposed to watch the sheep. That's your appointment. Here's a third lesson: Preparation must come before the opportunity. I went into electrical trades when I was 18 years old and had some success in it. Ultimately being promoted in various jobs, eventually I became a supervisor, then was promoted to Director of Facility at a HBCU. Upon leaving there another anointing promoted me to senior project manager for BOFA. As I was growing in Christ another push forward came as I continue to listen and stay humbled. I was again promoted to Senior Director and Construction project manager building a twenty-million-dollar facility for a church. God radically changed my life. I was seeking God more…and more however another lesson had to be learned. I went through divorce. This by far was the worst of all circumstances because I did not know what to do to salvage it. I knew how important it was, however, circumstance, the inability to address my own issues led me down a dark road. I lost myself in Christ. I thought I knew what I did not. I felt called into ministry early in my twenties, I was reminded of the call during and after divorce. I had to lean upon my faith in the middle of a shameful place that I did not want to be in. I felt like a complete failure. However, I made up my mind that I had to go back and trust the process. When I decided to go, I lost my job in the process. I knew God had called me to be a good man but most importantly a Christian Husband. I had to count it all as joy when I fell into divers' temptation knowing that this was the trying of my faith. After a time, it took its toll. I had left that job, because of seeking Gods face something amazing had happen. I heard the spirit talking to me and addressing my concerns, then leading me into a situation where I had to be completely honest with myself. It took another couple of years; I began to question if I was really doing what God had called me to do. Should I leave and go somewhere else? Why am I not getting the opportunity I deserve? Once I stopped questioning and complaining. God heard my sincere cry and plea to be right with him. The anointed appointment came in a way that is still unexplainable today. I landed a position with AECOM as Facility manager on a major account…for the last sixteen years. It was some years later… I heard Him say…" If I told you something and it came to pass…, what would you not do" I said nothing Lord...

A Reminder from God You Can Trust the Process

God was preparing me for the opportunity that would come. And this is what we see in David's life. David goes back to tend the sheep, and what happens? David Plays the Lyre… 1 Samuel 16:14-19 says, Now the Spirit of the Lord had departed from Saul, and an evil spirit from the Lord tormented him. Saul's attendants said to him, "See, an evil spirit from God is tormenting you. Let our lord command his servants here to search for someone who can play the lyre. He will play when the evil spirit from God comes on you, and you will feel better." So, Saul said to his attendants, "Find someone who plays well and bring him to me." One of the servants answered, "I have seen a son of Jesse of Bethlehem who knows how to play the lyre. He is a brave man and a warrior. He speaks well and is a fine-looking man. And the Lord is with him." Then Saul sent messengers to Jesse and said, "Send me your son David, who is with the sheep. It was while David was tending the sheep that he developed his ability to play the lyre and write music. In fact, it was while David was tending the sheep that he wrote Psalm 19:1, The heavens declare the glory of God; the skies proclaim the work of his hands. It may be that...the preparation had to come before the opportunity. Then, fast forward to the story of David and Goliath in 1 Samuel 17. David Kills Goliath... 1 Samuel 17:32-36 says, And David said to Saul, "Let no man's heart fail because of him. Your servant will go and fight with this Philistine. "And Saul said to David, "You are not able to go against this Philistine to fight with him, for you are but a youth, and he has been a man of war from his youth." But David said to Saul, "Your servant used to keep sheep for his father. And when there came a lion, or a bear, and took a lamb from the flock, I went after him and struck him and delivered it out of his mouth. And if he arose against me, I caught him by his beard and struck him and killed him. Your servant has struck down both lions and bears, and this uncircumcised Philistine shall be like one of them." Again, the preparation had to come before the opportunity. Above all... there are no short cuts! David had to prepare. If he had never mastered the lyre, he never would have been chosen to play for Saul, and Saul wouldn't have been familiar with him. If he had never killed the lion and the bear, Saul would not have let him face Goliath, and the Israelites wouldn't have accepted David as king. If David didn't prepare, he would have squandered the opportunity. But he did, and it led to him becoming king! You may be in a season of waiting. Maybe you have been waiting for a long time, and you are starting to wonder if God will ever bring about His promise. The fact is: You can trust the process. Let your faith be strengthened. Know that God is preparing you today for what He wants to do through you in the future. He's teaching you to trust him, to be bold in your faith, He's growing your character, and He's fine-tuning your gifts! Trust Him – the process is bringing about the promise!

Chapter 40

Touched in my Infirmities

The polarity of difference occurs in every aspect of our lives. It is the catalyst to the paradox of God in Christ and his  plan in all things. We cannot explain the unexplainable…. It's just what it is. To at least provide some clarity let's research infirmities. To the surprise of the Pharisees, Jesus came to help those who were lost. He taught that Gentiles they can have a relationship with their Jewish God. He healed many people of their illnesses and diseases. That's why I want to look at the definition of the word infirmity in Hebrew and Greek:

- An unsound or unhealthy state of the body; weakness; feebleness. Old age is subject to infirmities.
- Weakness of mind; failing; fault; foible. A friend should bear a friend's infirmities.
- Weakness of resolution.
- Any disease; malady; applied rather to chronic, than to violent diseases.
- Defect; imperfection; weakness; as the infirmities of a constitution of government."

There are many times where this word is translated as sick, but really means 'weak' in the context. For example: Joram is described as sick, but he's weak (2 Kings 8:29). In Song of Solomon 2:5, "sick with love" more than likely means "weak with passion". This word means lacking strength, weakness, or infirmity. It's translated into:

- Sickness (John 11:4)

224

- Infirmities (Matthew 8:17)
- Diseases (Acts 28:9)
- Weakness (1 Corinthians 2:3)

Paul notated in Galatian 4:13-14 the importance of grasping an understanding infirmity, because it is the catalyst for maintaining and embracing insightful mysteries of our walk in Christ. The infirmity which a man of resolution can keep under by his will (Proverbs 18:14) may be either moral or physical. In Luke 13:11 the woman's physical infirmity is ascribed to the influence of an evil spirit. The term spirit of infirmity occurs in Luke 13:11 specifically in the KJV. Here a woman who had been crippled for eighteen years is healed by Jesus on the Sabbath day. Luke says she has a "spirit of infirmity" or a "disabling spirit" (ESV) or a "sickness caused by a spirit" or is "crippled by a spirit". Quite simply then, this "spirit of infirmity" is a demon who caused the woman to be crippled for eighteen years. Consequentially… this is one part of the infirmities that can hinder our lives and that often time it is directly rooted in the morality of our action. The Bible is clear that spiritual warfare exists. Ephesians 6:12 says, "For our struggle is not against flesh and blood, but against the rulers, against the authorities, against the powers of this dark world and against the spiritual forces of evil in the heavenly realms." And, from Luke 13, evil spirits can sometimes cause physical maladies. Many of our ailments are simply caused by living in a fallen world, and there are many instances in Luke's gospel of people being healed of diseases with no mention of a demonic cause. There are a variety of reasons a person may be struggling with such things. No matter the specific cause of an infirmity, we can bring the problem to God in prayer. James 4:7–8 talks about resisting the devil and submitting to God. Prayer is one way to do this. James 5:16 says we should confess our sins to one another so that we can pray for healing. The major thing to observe from Luke 13:10–17 is the power and compassion of Jesus. In an instant, He overcame the disability this woman had been struggling with for eighteen years. He healed her on the Sabbath day, to the indignation of the Pharisees. He responded to her need with compassion, calling the woman a "daughter of Abraham" (verse 16) and highlighting how much God loved her and was willing to free her. Along these lines. Let's gather an understanding as to why we have our own infirmities based on Paul's thorn in the flesh, which is a figurative expression that refers to a messenger of Satan sent to buffet or torment him. There are different interpretations of what this messenger was, such as Paul's enemies who persecuted him and opposed his gospel, or a physical condition that affected his eyes, speech, or appearance. God allowed this thorn to keep Paul from becoming conceited because of his visions of heaven. Paul speaks of a "thorn in the flesh" in 2 Corinthians 12:7. He calls it "a messenger of Satan" that had a purpose of "torment." Many explanations have been put forward, but whether Paul is referring to a physical, spiritual, or emotional affliction or something else entirely has never been answered with satisfaction. Since he was not talking of a literal thorn, he must have been speaking metaphorically. Perhaps the more popular theories of the thorn's interpretation include temptation, a chronic eye problem, migraines, or something like what I had; bacteria pneumonia which almost killed me in 2021. All things considered, maybe the thorn refers to a person, such as Alexander the coppersmith, who did Paul "a great deal of harm" (2 Timothy 4:14). No one can say for sure what Paul's thorn in the flesh was, but it was a source of real pain in the apostle's life.

Paul clues us in concerning the thorn's purpose: "To keep me from becoming conceited because of these surpassingly great revelations." So, God's goal in allowing the thorn in the flesh was to keep Paul humble. Anyone who had encountered Jesus and was commissioned personally by Him (Acts 9:2-8) would, in his natural state, become "puffed up." Add to that the fact that Paul was moved by the Holy Spirit to write much of the New Testament, and it is easy to see how Paul could become "haughty" (KJV) or "exalted above measure" (NKJV) or "too proud" (NCV). He also…also says that the affliction came from or by a "messenger of Satan." Just as God allowed Satan to torment Job (Job 1:1-12), God allowed Satan to torment Paul for God's own good purpose. No one likes to live in pain. Paul sought the Lord three times to remove this source of pain from him (2 Corinthians 12:8). He had many good reasons why he should be pain-free: he could have a more effective ministry; he could reach more people with the gospel; he could glorify God even more! But the Lord was more concerned with building Paul's character and preventing pride. Instead of removing the problem, whatever it was, God gave Paul more overwhelming grace and more compensating strength. Paul learned that God's "power is made perfect in weakness" (verse 9). The exact nature of Paul's thorn in the flesh is uncertain. There's probably a good reason that we don't know. God likely wanted Paul's difficulty to be described in general enough terms to apply to any difficulty we may face now. Whether the "thorn" we struggle with today is physical, emotional, or spiritual, we can know that God has a purpose and that His grace is all-sufficient. Additionally…It would be difficult to walk in such power and not start to feel like you have arrived and living above all others; instead of walking one with the people you are to serve. Jesus exclaimed to us all that; "he that is greatest amongst you should be your servant." I have finally accepted the path, the pain, the sufferings and all the unexplainable and you can too.

Chapter 41

The Conclusion of the Matter

Jesus said to seek first the kingdom of God in His Sermon on the Mount (Matthew 6:33). The verse's meaning is as direct  as it sounds. We are to seek the things of God as a priority over the things of the world. Primarily, it means we are to seek the salvation that is inherent in the kingdom of God because it is of greater value than all the world's riches. Does this mean that we should neglect the reasonable and daily duties that help sustain our lives? Certainly not. But for the Christian, there should be a difference in attitude toward them. If we are taking care of God's business as a priority…seeking His salvation, living in obedience to Him, and sharing the good news of the kingdom with others…then He will take care of us as He promised. HIS WORD CANNOT LIE?

This means that…we can know we are following Christ by examining our own lives in reflection to His word. There are questions we can ask ourselves. For example…where do I primarily spend my energies? Is all my time and money spent on goods and activities that will certainly perish, or in the services of God…knowing the results live on for eternity? Those of us who have learned to truly put God first may then rest in this holy dynamic: "…and all these things will be given to you as well."

God has promised to provide for His own, supplying every need (Philippians 4:19), but His idea of what we need is often different from ours, and His timing will only occasionally meet our expectations. For example, we may see our need as riches or advancement, but God knows; we may need a time of poverty, loss, or solitude. When this happens, we are in good company. God loved both Job and Elijah, but He allowed Satan to absolutely pound Job (all under His watchful eye), and He let that evil woman, Jezebel, break the spirit of His own prophet Elijah (Job 1–2; 1 Kings 18–19). In both cases, God followed these trials with restoration and sustenance. Arguably…these "negative" aspects of the kingdom run counter to a heresy which is gaining ground around the world, the so-called "prosperity" gospel. A growing number of false teachers are gathering followers under the message "God wants you to be rich!" But that philosophy is not the counsel of the Bible…and it is certainly not the counsel of Matthew 6:33, which is not a formula for gaining wealth. It is a description of how God works. Jesus taught that our focus should be away from this world…its status and its lying allurements and placed upon the things of God's kingdom.

The Intermittent touch of God; Piercing the Darkness of a Broken but Enlightened Man. May these words provide you guidance and meditative counsel to your hearts that brings us closer to Christ Jesus. Amen…

Scriptures to Reflect on:

John 10:10 - The thief cometh not, but for to steal, and to kill, and to destroy I am come that they might have life, and that they might have it more abundantly.

Jeremiah 29:11 - For I know the thoughts that I think toward you, saith the LORD, thoughts of peace, and not of evil, to give you an expected end.

Romans 12:2 - And be not conformed to this world: but be ye transformed by the renewing of your mind, that ye may prove what is that good, and acceptable, and perfect, will of God.

Matthew 6:33 - But seek ye first the kingdom of God, and his righteousness; and all these things shall be added unto you.

Romans 15:13 - Now the God of hope fill you with all joy and peace in believing, that ye may abound in hope, through the power of the Holy Ghost.

Isaiah 58:11 - And the LORD shall guide thee continually, and satisfy thy soul in drought, and make fat thy bones: and thou shalt be like a watered garden, and like a spring of water, whose waters fail not.

Romans 5:8 - But God commended his love toward us, in that, while we were yet sinners, Christ died for us.

Proverbs 3:5-6 - Trust in the LORD with all thine heart; and lean not unto thine own understanding.   (Read More...)

Revelation 3:20 - Behold, I stand at the door, and knock: if any man hears my voice, and open the door, I will come into him, and will sup with him, and he with me.

Ephesians 2:8-9 - For by grace are ye saved through faith; and that not of yourselves: it is the gift of God: (Read More...)

Romans 10:13 - For whosoever shall call upon the name of the Lord shall be saved.

John 3:16 - For God so loved the world, that he gave his only begotten Son, that whosoever believeth in him should not perish, but have everlasting life.

Psalms 1:1-3 - Blessed is the man that walketh not in the counsel of the ungodly, nor stand in the way of sinners, nor sit in the seat of the scornful. (Read More...)

Romans 6:23 - For the wages of sin is death; but the gift of God is eternal life through Jesus Christ our Lord.

Acts 2:38 - Then Peter said unto them, Repent, and be baptized every one of you in the name of Jesus Christ for the remission of sins, and ye shall receive the gift of the Holy Ghost.

1 Corinthians 2:9 - But as it is written, Eye hath not seen, nor ear heard, neither have entered the heart of man, the things which God hath prepared for them that love him.

John 1:12 - But as many as received him, to them gave the power to become the sons of God, even to them that believe on his name:

Psalms 119:12-16 - Blessed art thou, O LORD: teach me thy statutes. (Read More...)

1 Timothy 6:18-19 - That they do good, that they be rich in good works, ready to distribute, willing to communicate; (Read More...)

John 8:32 - And ye shall know the truth, and the truth shall make you free.

Psalms 139:13 - 127:16 - For thou hast possessed my reins: thou hast covered me in my mother's womb.   (Read More...)

James 4:7 - Submit yourselves therefore to God. Resist the devil, and he will flee from you.

Philippians 4:19 - But my God shall supply all your need according to his riches in glory by Christ Jesus.

Jude 1:24

Unto him who can keep us from falling

THE END

NOTES: